Nourishing Meals
on
Camper Wheels

. . . and

Yoga *at the* Rest Stop

Katie Carter NC., CYT

Printed in the United States of America.
Wild Grown Press
ISBN # 978-0-578-45325-5

Contact the author:
katiecarterwellness@gmail.com
or www.katiecarterwellness.com

*For Wild Ranger Bill,
my sexy chauffeur
and seeker of wilderness*

Table *of* Contents

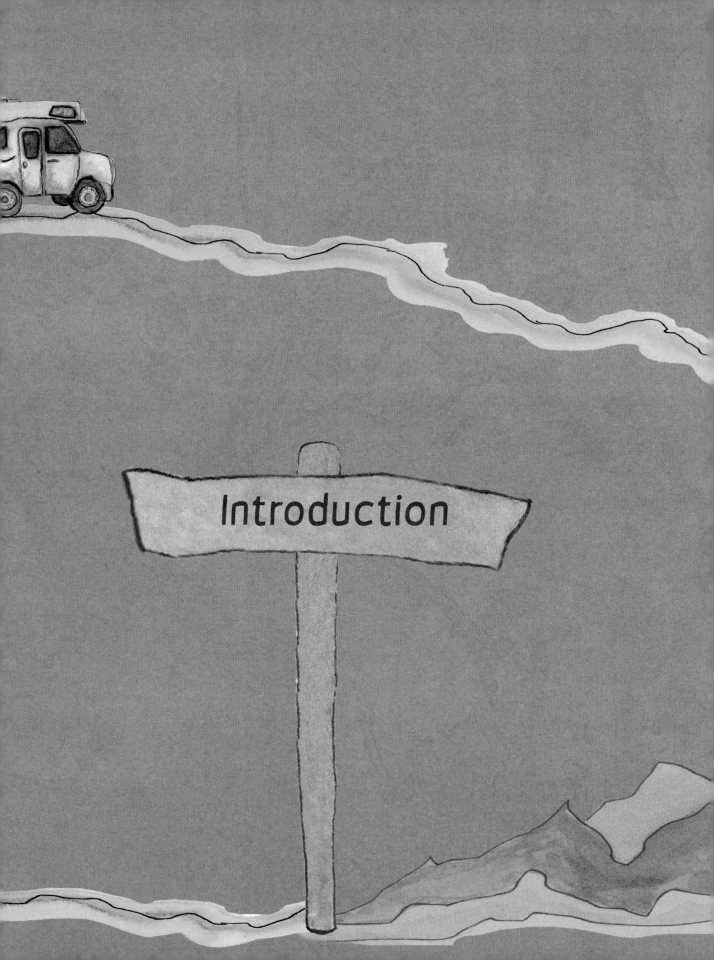

Introduction

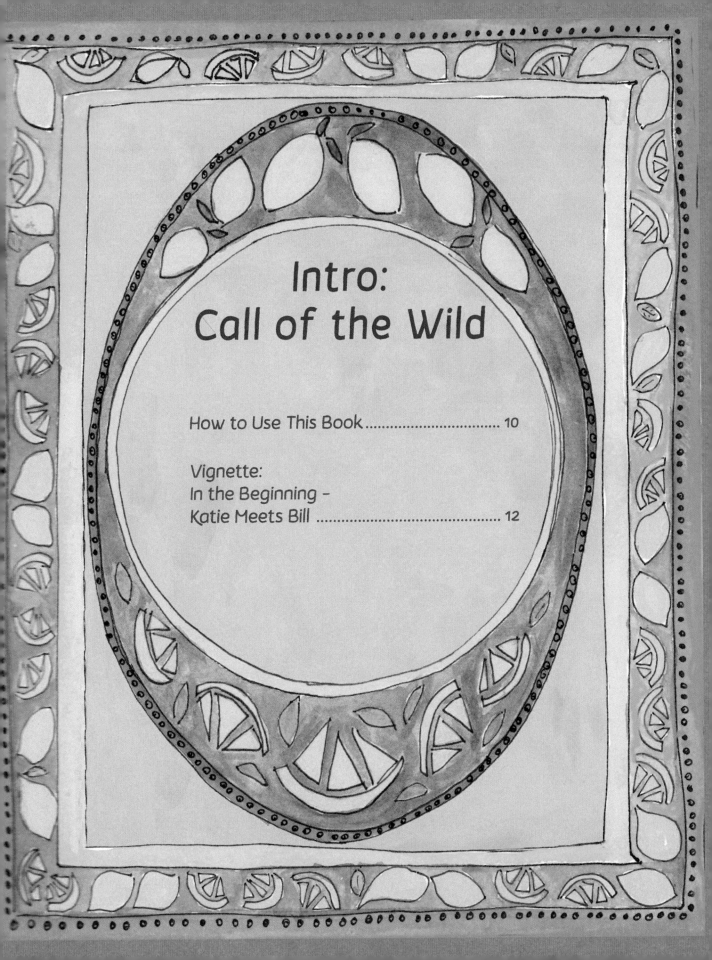

Intro:
Call of the Wild

Call of the Wild

"We live in a wonderful world full of beauty, charm, and adventure. There is no end to the adventures we can have, if we seek them with our heart and mind wide open." –Jawaharial Nehru

Our friends call my husband Wild Ranger Bill. Lucky me - I've been married to this seeker of wilderness for over 40 years and we both love to travel and explore "wilderness" in our own way.

Bill believes the majestic and untamed territories in the United States are slowly diminishing and, before they become extinct, he wants to experience as many wild places as he can.

I feel lucky to be surrounded by beautiful scenery with my own sexy chauffeur in our traveling camper. I could feel "stuck" in the solitude of the back-country without the conveniences of home or close girlfriend time, but I've learned to explore and express my own inner wilderness in fulfilling ways. When we started traveling sans kids, I found a wild sense of creativity emerging while cooking, practicing yoga, journaling, making art or dancing in nature.

I'm writing this book to share my passion for creating healthy, tasty, gluten-free whole-food meals in my tiny kitchen on the road. I don't claim to be a gourmet chef, but you might call me an inspiring and unconventional campfire cook.

As a certified nutrition consultant, I'm focused on healthy, whole-food, TASTY

meals that are easy to make while camping. Not only will you find my favorite travel recipes in this book, you'll also be blessed with my other passion.

I've been practicing and teaching yoga for over 20 years. As my sons will testify, I like to practice at the rest stop, in airports and on top of picnic tables in a campground. I will share some of the best postures that can be practiced anywhere for travelers who spend a day driving, hiking, kayaking or lounging at the beach.

I believe yoga is so much more than the physical postures. As a seasoned yoga teacher, I love to help folks take their yoga "philosophy" off the mat and into their daily lives. You will notice this philosophy is like a golden thread running throughout this book, encouraging you to make the most of your travels through life.

With an open heart and mind I embrace a healthy diet and lifestyle. With an open heart and mind I embrace being on vacation.

When traveling I make a conscious effort to blend these mindsets because we all like to shift into "vacation mode" when we take time off. Yes we've worked hard and now it's time to party! We're on VACATION! Does that mean bending ALL the rules? Does it mean we can eat and drink "forbidden foods"?

As I age with more wisdom, it's important to me to remain healthy even on vacation. I don't recover from any form of abuse, as quickly as I use to. My husband Bill is NOT gluten sensitive but he loves all the meals I create and if he has a strong desire for gluten foods, we stop at a bakery or he orders his favorite treats when we eat out. We just don't use camping as an excuse to eat marshmallows and other junk foods.

Whether you're camping in a car, truck, van, motor home or trailer this book has recipes for healthy meals and tips to improve or maintain your health while exploring the Great Outdoors.

Make your trip an awesome, memorable experience instead of returning home 5 lbs. heavier and needing a detox. Cheers to having healthy adventures on the road with ***Nourishing Meals on Camper Wheels and Yoga at the Rest Stop***!

How to Use this Book

When I was a kid our family played a traveling alphabet game in the car. It went like this:

1st player: I'm going on a trip and I'm taking an Apple,

2nd player: I'm going on a trip and I'm taking an Apple and a Badminton set,

3rd player: I'm going on a trip and I'm taking an Apple, a Badminton Set, and Crackers!!!

I chuckle now as I enter the age of "senior moments" and realize this is a great game to keep my brain alert!!!

But seriously: What ARE you going to take on your trip?

Whether you're camping in a car, van, truck, trailer or RV, this book will tell you what to bring, so you can have a great trip, great food and a healthy, happy body.

When planning a road trip most of us may spend hours studying maps and points of interest to visit. But we may get stumped when it comes to planning delicious, yet simple meals, stocking our camp kitchens with all we will need, and putting together a really good natural first aid kit.

Here's what I suggest:

1) Start by browsing through this book to find inspiration in the photographs, recipes and writings of meals, landscapes, yoga or camping activities.

2) Pick out a few favorites dishes that appeal to your taste buds.

In some recipes I swap inflammatory ingredients (foods that cause inflammation and ill health—see the list of inflammatory foods on page 34) and replace them with healthy low-carb options. Of course, you may opt to stock your favorite higher-carb foods like breads, cookies, scones and pasta. But you'll notice I'm not a big fan of sugar, bread, baked goods or just about anything

made with wheat flour. I prefer to eat gluten-free, so I swap wheat for coconut or arrowroot flour when possible. You may be pleasantly surprised how delicious gluten free pancakes (page 64), vegetable frittata with sweet potato crust (page 70) or fresh fruit and chocolate fondue can taste.

3) As far as practicing yoga at the rest stop or campground, no props are necessary. You can bring a yoga strap (or a bathrobe tie or belt will work). A yoga mat is optional. You can always place a towel on top of the picnic table at a campsite.

And don't forget to bring an open heart and
open mind on your trip.

The camping experience can be really fun and memorable when we plan ahead. Take time to plan meals, shop for food, prepare a few secret sauces or dips before you leave and stock those camper cupboards. You'll be happy you did!

"Focus on the journey, not the destination. Joy is found not in finishing an activity but in doing it."

–Greg Anderson

In the Beginning - Katie meets Bill

I grew up in the suburbs of Milwaukee, Wisconsin.

My only memory of camping with my "city folk" family was on a trip to the beautiful recreational peninsula of Door County, WI. We had a big family argument setting up the tent; the boom box was blasting; we ate burnt hotdogs on a stick and I fell asleep with gooey bits of marshmallow smeared all over my face and hands.

Needless to say we never tried camping again.

Before heading to college I was drawn to a book called **Back to the Land**. It inspired a dream to someday buy property, build a house and learn to survive with the rhythms of nature.

I was a country girl at heart.

Fast forward.... It's 1975 and I've just graduated from University of Wisconsin. Before delivering a "drive–away car" to California with two girlfriends, we bought sleeping bags, backpacks and a tent at the grand opening of Milwaukee's first REI. We thought we knew what we were doing. After dropping the car off in Monterey, CA, with packs on our backs, we hitchhiked (Yes remember it's 1975) down Highway 1 to Pfeiffer State Park in Big Sur, CA. A "hippie couple" in a Volkswagen van with beads hanging in the windows picked us up. I'm sure they were chuckling as they turned us on to a spectacular ride to the park, complete with smoking a big, fat joint. Wowie! Zowie! We were so innocent and thrilled by our first California experience. That night three enchanted girls slept in new sleeping bags inside a pup tent after eating ramen noodles and tuna fish for dinner.

The next day, now carless, we hiked 2 ½ miles to a cold and foggy beach. "Where are the California surfers?" we naively asked. Dressed in bikini tops, cut offs and not a soul on the beach, we found a protected sand dune to shield us from the wind. Finally two guys came walking close to the surf. With a friendly

smile I waved at them as they continued to walk down the beach.

On their way back they headed right toward our secluded spot.

GIRLFRIENDS: "Katie, why did you wave at them? Now they're coming up here."

ME: "Shut up, maybe they have a car and can drive us back to the campground."

The two native Californians had been exploring hot springs along the coast. They became curious enough to check out three crazy young women wearing bikini tops on a freezing cold day. Imagine the picture. After talking for hours, we finally invited them back to our campsite for dinner - if they would drive. Now what 24-year-old guy wouldn't want to do that?

To shorten this fairytale story that could only happen in California – one of those guys with a ponytail named Bill became my husband in 1976. We've been married for 43 years and live in Northern California on 5 acres in the home we built ourselves!

And we both still love to play "house" and cook whole food meals on camper wheels.

Chapter 1

1
Camping as Mind-Body Medicine

Camping as Mind-Body Medicine

"There is a love of wild nature in everybody, an ancient mother-love showing itself whether recognized or not, and however covered by cares and duties."
–John Muir

While raising two active sons, our family loved camping vacations. Not only did it fit our budget, camping in the desert, mountains or coast was definitely our preferred way to explore new territory. It guaranteed quality time together and allowed us to forget about work and school.

Despite the occasional hard work of camping with children, the joy of witnessing your child discover the wonders of nature makes it all worthwhile. Our sons loved picking out the campsite, exploring the campground on their bikes, gathering and splitting wood for the campfire, hiking to the top of a mountain, swimming in icy glacier lakes and rivers and sleeping in the top bunk of the camper van. To this day, our boys, now grown men, continue to thrive in the great outdoors.

When Bill and I became empty nesters, our camping trips became "healing retreats" from the hectic work of running our own businesses. After being diagnosed with adrenal fatigue—feeling wired but tired, unable to get restful sleep, anxious and dependent on caffeine—I knew I needed to slow down to regain my energy and find my natural rhythm.

My healing began on a winter camping trip to Death Valley. I wrote in my journal

that I was looking forward to doing "nothing" in the "Zen" environment of the desert. After settling into a secluded campsite, we spent our days exploring, reading, making art and sleeping like babies under the cool night skies. Our desert campfire ignited my internal flame to create mandalas and symbols out of rocks. I prepared healing whole food meals each day and by the end of the week, I was beginning to feel like Katie again.

Camping provides profound healing benefits for people of all ages and lifestyles, making it a "whole food" healing tonic for body, mind, heart and spirit.

Here are some of the many healing benefits of camping:

- **SIMPLIFY:** Camping brings us back to our basic needs, helping us to realize we don't really need many of the things we often get caught up in.

- **FEEL EMPOWERED:** Camping also gets us in touch with basic survival skills, such as how to make a fire and dig a hole for an outhouse. This is empowering and enlivening.

- **SLOW DOWN:** Camping slows things down and unhooks us from a need for constant stimulation. With no electronic screen time (computers, TVs, video games, or cell phones), we begin to explore our surroundings and our senses become heightened. A quiet mind allows us to hear, smell, touch and see things we would never experience on Facebook or Netflix. And these things nourish us far more deeply.

- **APPRECIATION:** We appreciate the simple things in life – staying dry during a rainstorm, watching the flames of a fire, making art with rocks.

- **SOUND SLEEP:** Our sleep improves by getting in sync with circadian rhythms. Our internal body clock is reset by sunlight and temperature that tells the body when to sleep, rise and eat. Spending time outside surrounded by natural light, melatonin levels (the hormone that signals sleep) rise, and falling asleep becomes easier. The fresh air and exercise we get while camping help with this too.

- **GROUNDING OR EARTHING:** We get "earthed" by simply walking outside barefoot or lying on the ground. The Earth is actually a giant battery filled with positive and negative electrons. When skin is exposed to sunlight, it transfers negative electrons from earth into our body. Research has proven that these electrons help decrease inflammation, reduce pain, promote healthy sleep and reduce heart disease. Negative ions are referred to as "nature's antidepressants" and have a relaxing and healing effect. Just go and lie or walk barefoot on the ground!

- **FRESH AIR:** Inhale, exhale! Energize! Camping gives us a break from indoor air that is filled with invisible chemicals and plastics often trapped in by airtight insulation, windows and doors.

- **VITAMIN D:** Spending time in sunlight helps our body produce natural vitamin D. This vital pre-hormone is responsible for many aspects of health. When it is deficient, it has been linked to various types of cancer and obesity, as well as mental disorders and other health problems.

- **HUMAN INTERACTION:** It is easy to find common ground when meeting folks on a trail, at a campground, or Ranger station. Nature is the great mediator for all types of people. Whether it is sharing a campfire recipe, story or advice about our environment, communicating with others in the Great Outdoors can be a wonderful bonding experience.

This book is all about living a "whole foods" lifestyle on the road. With a little effort and planning, our trips can be healing tonics for whatever ails us.

"Log off, shut down and get outside!" Anonymous

Our Time Line of Camping Vehicles

Our very first camping rig was a classic 1978 VW camper van. It had a pop-top allowing my husband to stand tall in the back and create space for a bunk bed above our queen bed. Our young sons loved sleeping on the top bunk and I remember listening to them giggle themselves to sleep. The cook stove was set up on a platform outside the side door when we stopped for the day. It was fun cooking outside but not very convenient when it rained.

After our sons left home, we upgraded to a **1996 Ford Adventure-wagon** hand built in Fort Bragg, CA. This vehicle was roomier, had a beautiful teak interior and was finished like a yacht. We added solar panels, had a better kitchen layout and refrigerator and the engine was in great shape.

We enjoyed the Ford van for 5 years before we purchased our current DREAM vehicle—a custom built, 4-wheel drive, **Tiger Pro-van**. Only 19 feet long, the TIGER has a decadent little "wet" bathroom, which means everything gets wet including sink, shower and toilet when we shower. We also have a great dining space and two sleeping areas – a queen bed above the cab and a single bed for a grandkid or wife with hot flashes. The best part is our really big refrigerator (compared to most campers) stocked full of organic, pasture raised, whole foods and premade dressings and secret sauces.

One of our first adventures boondocking in Death Valley was in our 1996 Ford Adventure Wagon.

It's a Food Revolution!

If you're reading this book, I assume you've noticed a food revolution going on. How can you NOT notice the quality and quantity of organic produce and grass fed meats popping up in conventional grocery stores, big box stores and of course health food stores and local farmer's market?

Hey folks we're witnessing a Food Revolution!!!!

According to Wikipedia: "[a] revolution is a fundamental change in political power or organizational structures that takes place in a relatively short period of time when the population rises up in revolt against the current authorities."

This movement is spirited by the philosophy of the Greek physician and Father of Western Medicine Hippocrates (460–370 B.C.) who said:

"Let food be thy medicine and medicine be thy food."

As the American diet became more processed and the food industry tricked us into believing we'd find freedom "out of the kitchen," we all witnessed our health and well-being disintegrate. Most Americans opted for quick, inexpensive, GMO and processed food whether at home, on the road or eating out in restaurants.

Somewhere along our time line of food consumption we forgot (for about 50-70 years while the food industry took over) what we now understand and BELIEVE to be true:

Food can heal our bodies and ultimately by the way it's grown, raised and distributed, food can heal our world!!!

Food is information that controls our gene expression, hormones, and metabolism. When consumed, it signals hormones (chemical messengers secreted by glands into blood) and neurotransmitters (chemical messages secreted instantly through our nervous system) to activate certain reactions in our body. The right foods can:

- Change the way our genes express themselves

- Lower inflammation

- Re-build cell membranes, bones, hormones and all organs

- Assist our liver in filtering out toxins

- Decrease our chances of developing a chronic disease

- And help us grow older with grace and dignity

The Food Revolution gained some attention when the "Baby Boomers" began leaving the cities and getting "back to the land". But I think the most important change happened when we realized we needed to get Back to the Kitchen (and garden if we can) and grow and cook our own food. Today it's a lot easier to find the most nutritious food, recipes and inspiration to satisfy our individual nutrition needs and our longing for one of life's greatest pleasures – EATING!!!!

"I did then what I knew how to do....
Now that I know better, I do better."
—Maya Angelou

Our Spirit Guide

"Everyone wants to live on top of the mountain, but all the happiness and growth occurs while you're climbing it." —Andy Rooney

I believe we have Spirit helpers looking after us, here to guide, protect and support us. They may show up as God-like energy, angels, our higher self, ancestors, power animals or totems. When the time is right, they gently remind us of our connection to divine energy and can be called upon to help us on our soul journey.

We met one spirit guide while camping on the coast of Northern California at Usal Beach. One morning I took Ginger, our mellow rescue dog for a walk. Most of the time, she was unleashed, but something had me put her leash back on as we came near our campsite. This turned out to be a good thing. Coming into the site, we saw a huge elk with giant antlers standing 20 feet from our camper.

Bill grabbed his camera. Ginger madly tugged on her rope. The elk just continued munching on green shrubs. OH! What a magical moment!

Once Ginger realized this great beast was friendly, she quieted down. I watched entranced as Mr. Elk sauntered down the beach, commanding respect from all the other campers and un-tethered dogs. He was definitely King of this campground.

"I believe when we randomly encounter animals on our path they have a distinct message or medicine to share with us."

Elk Medicine teaches us that it's not necessary to be the first one to reach a goal. It's more essential to pace ourselves, increase our stamina, and arrive without being burned out. Except at mating time, Elk honor the company of their own gender. This message teaches us to seek connection with brother-

hood and sisterhood, to air feelings in safety and overcome potential competition and jealousy of our own sex.

Thank you Mr. Elk! While writing this book I held Elk medicine close to my heart. I invite you, fellow campers, to pace yourself while camping, cooking, eating, hiking, and exploring the great outdoors. Being in nature has a way of reminding us to slow down, relax and mindfully witness the great outdoors. There's no need to hurry. It's a great time to explore new adventures and return home replenished.

Chapter 2

2
Camp Cook Sutras

Camp Cook Sutras

Sutra – A rule or guideline in Sanskrit literature.

The word "sutra" has another meaning as well. Sutra is related to the word "suture" or threads that string or sew things together. According to ancient yoga texts, the Yoga Sutras weave together the warp (threads that run up and down) and weft (threads that weave across the warp – over under, over under) of our material and spiritual lives.

Yoga Sutras – An ancient spiritual text that weaves a beautiful tapestry of essential wisdom to help us to know our True Selves.

Yoga Sutra # 1

"With humility (an open heart and mind) we embrace the sacred study of Yoga."

CAMP COOK SUTRAS

I invite you to embrace the spirit of the Yoga Sutra #1 (an open heart and mind) while cooking and traveling on the road.

My camp cook guidelines weave a strong foundational "warp" (healthy whole foods) with a mystical "weft" (an open heart and mind) to create a tapestry of healthy, delicious meals that cultivate peace, love and true enjoyment.

Traditions among family and friends can often play a major part in planning our camp trip meals, so that we pack the same things we always have. In this book I want to dispel the myth that camp cooking is just a challenging necessity to keep us fueled for a fun weekend, or that outdoor cooking means hot dogs, energy breakfast bars, tuna fish or ramen noodles in a foam cup.

I want to inspire you to create healthy, creative, whole food meals!

Taking a vacation in the great outdoors can be one of life's greatest pleasures as well as a healing tonic for whatever ails us. But even a long weekend can turn into a disaster if we don't plan ahead and make mindful choices, including about

food. Many folks compromise their meals for the experience of sleeping under the stars, breathing clean air and connecting to nature. But you don't have to leave the healthy (and yummy!) eating at home in order to have a good time in the outdoors.

So, here are the Camp Cook Sutras, my guidelines to help you choose wisely when planning your meals on the road:

1.   **Buy Organic** – as much as possible! I recommend you look for these qualities in the food you buy: organic, grass-fed, pasture-raised, wild-caught, fresh, and gluten–free. Why are fresh organic whole foods good for us? They're not stripped of their essential nutrients through processing, contain more fiber and are rich in phytochemicals to help protect us and prevent disease. (If we run out of fresh produce while on the road, I use my smart phone to Google the nearest health food store.)

2.   **Stock the Basics** - In general, foods fall in to two categories: inflammatory and anti-inflammatory. Research and countless studies prove that inflammation is at the root of all chronic illness. The foods listed below are all anti-inflammatory, unless stated. Find my list of inflammatory foods to avoid or decrease on page 34.

Browse through the recipes and choose appealing and practical meals that can be prepared in your camp kitchen. Keep in mind the size of your refrigerator or cooler and how much space you have to stock basic cupboard ingredients.

From the lists to follow, pick your favorite items and/or those you need for the recipes you have chosen.

3. Protein - for the Cupboard:

   a. Canned, wild-caught salmon

   b. Sardines

   c. Smoked oysters

   d. Beef or turkey jerky

   e. Chicken broth

   f. Protein energy bars for hiking

   g. Nuts and seeds

   h. Ziploc bag or jar of vegan protein powder

4. Refrigerator Protein:

   a. Smoked turkey, ham, or sliced turkey or chicken

   b. Favorite cheeses (organic, raw and goat or sheep cheeses are optimal)

   c. Plain, organic, full-fat goat or cow yogurt, kefir or crème fraîche (cultured sour cream)

   d. Eggs (pasture raised) - hard boil a few before your trip

   e. ½ to 1 cup fresh ground flax seeds (rich in protein)

5. Freezer protein:

   a. Turkey, pork or chicken sausage or meatballs

   b. Bacon or organic breakfast sausage

   c. One or two grass-fed steaks, chicken, pork tenderloin, fresh salmon, or steelhead trout or any other favorite animal protein

6. Fats and oils

   a. **For the cupboard**: olive oil, coconut oil, avocados, can of full-fat coconut milk

      b. **Refrigerator fats**: olives, pastured, cultured & unsalted butter, ghee for vegans, crème fraîche (See cheese and yogurt choices under refrigerator proteins.)

7. Carbohydrates

a. **Vegetables:** onions, garlic, leeks, asparagus, broccoli, cauliflower, sweet potato, yams, potatoes, leafy greens, peppers, or any seasonal vegetable

b. **Cultured and fermented foods**: such as full-fat plain yogurt, butter, raw pickles, sauerkraut, kombucha, kimchi, raw apple cider vinegar. These contain live cultures (friendly bacteria) that assist our digestion to fully absorb nutrients.

c. **Grains / legumes**: quinoa, gluten-free rolled oats, canned black beans, or refried beans, homemade hummus or store bought organic. (Note: When my resilience is low, I avoid all grains and legumes because they can promote inflammation.)

d. **Packaged foods**: Gluten-free flours (I like cassava, arrowroot, almond and coconut flour), Thai kitchen rice noodles or Thai Kitchen curry sauce, Pad Thai (or another Thai favorite package food), canned coconut milk

e. **Fruits**: lemons, limes, berries, oranges, mango, apples, pears, and dried fruit. Be sure to bring fruits in season.

8. Condiments

a. Baking soda – not just for baking but helps buffer an acid stomach and when made into a paste with water helps relieve bug bites and stings (see first aid, page 177)

b. Fish sauce – especially if you like Thai food

c. Sriracha Sauce

d. Prepared horseradish

e. Gluten-Free Hoisin Sauce by Premier Japan

f. Avocado mayonnaise (I like Sir Kensington's or Primal Kitchen mayo)

g. Apple cider and balsamic vinegar

h. Sea salt (I like Redmond's Real Sea Salt)

i. Gomasio with Seaweed (By Eden contains sesame seeds, seaweed and sea salt)

j. Whole black pepper in grinder

k. Essential oils – I love these and since they pack so small I sometimes season with food-grade-only, pure essential oils, such as lime, lemongrass, peppermint and cinnamon. (See more about essential oils on page 138.)

9. Beverages

a. Mineral water

b. Kombucha tea

c. Powdered Matcha green tea

d. Coffee or decaf grounds

e. SPORTea® by UPP Ultimate performance products

10. **SPECIAL KITCHEN TOOLS**

a. Heavy duty aluminum foil – great for foil packet meals

b. Parchment paper

c. Really good knives, tongs, pot holder and kitchen scissors

d. Hand held Progressive adjust-a-slice & julienne mandolin—my absolutely most favorite tool!

e. Dutch Oven - try my Dutch Oven Apple Crisp, page 152

f. Blender cup - Used to mix dressings, marinades, and Grab and Go Quick Breakfast Smoothie, page 61

g. Citrus juice reamer – another favorite that has taken the place of a juice squeezer. You must try this efficient tool!

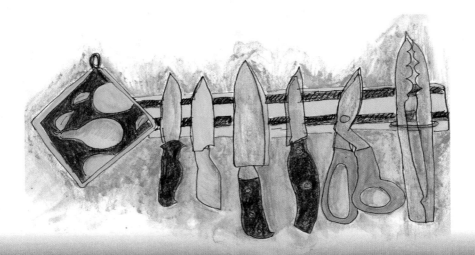

Inflammatory Foods to Avoid or Decrease:

1. **HARMFUL CHEMICALS LIKE HERBICIDES,** pesticides and GMO's (genetically modified organisms) usually found in conventionally-grown produce. Reduce your exposure to these poisons by choosing organically grown whenever possible. Yes, buying organic can be more expensive, but the nutrient profile of organic produce versus conventionally-grown is incomparable. Conventionally-grown foods lack nutrients and are filled with chemicals.

2. **SEED OILS** including soybean, canola, corn, safflower, sunflower and cottonseed oils. These oils can oxidize easily and turn rancid when heated.

3. **LOW-FAT AND SKIM MILK DAIRY PRODUCTS.** Without the butterfat in dairy, low-fat foods convert to sugar very quickly. Full-fat dairy converts to sugar slowly because the butterfat takes longer to breakdown.

4. **SUGAR** - Consume only 20-40 grams/day, from any food you purchase in a package, bottle or box. Bacteria, inflammation, and cancer cells love sugar; it is their main food source. Sugar fertilizes bad bacteria and raises blood sugar levels. Watch for hidden sugars. Read food labels carefully. Look at the grams of sugar in foods you purchase and if one serving has more that 5 grams of sugar – put it back! Words ending in **–ose** indicate sugar: Sucrose, maltose, lactose, and fructose. All carbohydrates turn to sugar or glucose. Be cautious with high carbohydrate snack foods – pretzels, chips, crackers, cookies, cakes, etc.

    Also be cautious of eating excess fruits or starchy carbs (sweet potatoes, potatoes, corn, beets, winter squash). These foods do contain plenty of fiber to slow the conversion to sugar but don't go overboard.

5. **GLUTEN, DAIRY, SOY, PEANUTS, CORN AND ALL GRAINS** – these foods are known to cause inflammation in some folks. Personally I avoid gluten 100%, but have less of a reaction to full-fat organic dairy, soy, peanuts, rice, oats and corn. I consume these foods cautiously and avoid when I feel my resilience is low.

STRESS - especially when it comes to cooking and eating, stress can be a major cause of inflammation in the body. I believe all things are energetically connected and the food we prepare will reflect the mood we're in. The best mental state is kindness. Check in with yourself before cooking or eating and bring yourself into a relaxed and happy place that will transfer through your food. If you're stressed about food not being organic, let it go! Stress is absolutely the WORST toxin that ultimately causes inflammation and illness.

A Science Lesson in Gluten Sensitivity

When humans started eating grains, they were carefully soaked and sprouted to break down the gluten present making them easier to digest and assimilate. Our soils use to be organic, free of pesticides and herbicides and grains were not genetically modified. Crops were rotated on different areas of land and the soil had time to replenish trace minerals.

Gluten is the protein found in wheat, barley, rye and often oats. It can trigger celiac disease, a life–threatening gut condition. Other people display gluten sensitivity that might show up as brain fog, skin problems, joint pain, or inflammation anywhere in the body. And some folks have no symptoms at all from eating gluten.

Gluten sensitivity or intolerance of any food really depends on 3 factors:
1. The health of your gastrointestinal tract
2. The behavior of your micro biome (friendly bacteria)
3. The strength of your immune function

Since the late 1980's commercial wheat has been genetically modified. The fields are drenched with Round Up seven days before harvest as a drying agent. The unique way that individual body's react to Round Up is just one of the main culprits behind stomach symptoms. (Round Up contains glyphosphate and labeled in California as cancer causing.) And this is probably why you can eat bread in Italy and France symptom free but perhaps have GI problems when eaten in the U.S.

Does this mean that you can never have a piece of bread, pasta or pizza ever again? And is gluten really that bad for you? Well that will have to be your choice, and you'll need to experiment and decide if it's worth it to you.

Solutions for lightening your load of gluten!

1.   Gluten-free isn't always the best choice but it has become the new buzz word. Yes, gluten is a major cause of some health issues, but there's a downside to gluten-free. The Food Industry adds factory-made stuff to gluten-free products (so they have a longer shelf life) and a gluten-free cookie is still a cookie. Gluten-free products are made from processed gluten-free grains that convert to sugar quickly.

2.   Try grain-free tortillas made from cassava and almond flour. The brand Siete makes a good one that I like.

3.   Add ½ cup of these starchy carbs to your meals: beets, carrots, winter squash and cooked tubers (sweet potatoes, yams, potatoes or plantains). You'll feel satiated and more grounded by eating root vegetables and small portions of dense, starchy carbohydrates. Bonus: they're loaded with FIBER!

4.   Don't depend on the food industry to feed us. They could care less about our health and more about the money to be made.

5.   Be mindful of what ingredients you put into your body. Substitute ingredients in my recipes (with other whole foods) to suit your tastes.

6.   Look at cooking with whole foods as an art form! It can be an expression of your creativity and innovation.

My Personal Health Story

I became gluten-free and "selective dairy-free" when one of my sons was diagnosed with Akylosing Spondylitis (a rare form of Rheumatoid arthritis). A functional medicine doctor wisely advised him to eliminate gluten, dairy, grains, legumes and sugar (basically a Paleo diet). He also made some lifestyle changes (like no more sitting all day at a desk job) to improve his health. His inflammation cooled down eventually and through years of experimentation he has learned what foods and lifestyle his body needs to thrive.

At the same time, I was noticing my finger joints were swollen and achy. I began eliminating gluten, dairy, grains and legumes and this diet proved beneficial for me too. BINGO! My inflammation disappeared and only resurfaces if my life is stressed and I over-consume some of MY inflammatory foods (for me it's gluten, commercial dairy, un-soaked grains and legumes). I was very strict on the elimination diet for about 3 months and my digestion and inflammation improved immensely.

I was so impressed with using "Food as Medicine" that I made a life-changing decision to go back to school. At 56, I enrolled at Hawthorn University to become a certified holistic nutrition consultant and learn the science behind my discoveries.

Upon graduating, I sold Wild Mountain Yoga Center, the yoga studio I founded and taught at for 15 years, and opened my private practice, Katie Carter Wellness, providing holistic nutrition consulting and yoga classes.

And now that I don't own a yoga studio, Bill and I have a lot more free time to hit the road with our camper and explore the great outdoors!

Son Logan helping with my garden harvest

Chapter 3

3
Dressings, Dips, Salsas & Chutneys

Secret Sauces: *Dressings, Dips, Salsas and Chutneys*

If you fail to plan then plan to fail.

Without a doubt, preparing one or two of these secret sauces, marinades or condiments before your trip, will transform travel meals into a decadent dining experience. Campground neighbors will salivate, as they smell the aroma of these delicious recipes. The KEY here is to Plan Ahead.

If you make just one or two of these tasty sauces before your trip, you will be VERY grateful!!!!

Berry Ginger Chutney

This could be a make-ahead chutney or easy enough to prepare in your tiny kitchen. Great with ethnic food (Indian, Thai or Mediterranean), on savory pancakes, on grilled pork tenderloin, or serve as an appetizer with goat cheese and gluten-free crackers. You can be super creative with ingredients.

I have used strawberries, sliced kumquats, and soaked dried figs for the mixed berries along with all the other ingredients and it was yummy. Don't be afraid to use any fruit on hand.

- 1 medium red onion chopped
- 4 cloves garlic sliced
- 1 Tbsp. coconut oil
- 2 cups mixed berries
- 1 lemon zested and juiced
- 2-3 Tbsp. honey
- 1 inch chunk ginger sliced thin
- 3 Tbsp. apple cider vinegar

1. Sauté chopped red onion and garlic slices in coconut oil until soft.

2. Add mixed berries, lemon zest & juice, honey, ginger slices and apple cider vinegar.

3. Let simmer about 20 minutes until it looks like perfect chutney.

Peach Kumquat Salsa

A real crowd pleaser. If you can find kumquats locally, this salsa will deliver the ZING you're looking for. I serve this with a variety of meals and double the recipe if I have enough fixings. The list of ingredients seems long, but salsas are easy to make. Great on grilled fish, pork, chicken, or egg dishes. Be sure to try it on fish tacos, page 108.

- 1 green onion: both green and white parts chopped fine
- ½ red pepper, chopped
- ½ seeded jalapeño or ½ tsp. red pepper flakes or more to taste
- 2 Tbsp. lime juice
- 1 ½ tsp. ginger, finely grated
- 2 Tbsp. cilantro
- 6–8 kumquats cut in half (or swap for 1–3 tsp. grated orange rind), remove seeds, then finely chop.
- 1 whole peach, nectarine or mango, or ½ pineapple, chopped
- 1 tsp. toasted sesame oil
- Salt & pepper to taste

1. Mix all ingredients and let sit to marinate for 20 minutes.

Nutrition Tip

Kumquats are sweet, tart little oval shaped fruit with an amazing storehouse of vitamins, minerals and antioxidants that can boost your immune system, bone health and energy levels. I add thin, seeded slices of kumquats to salads, smoothies, salsas and desserts for an incredible BURST of flavor! Eat the whole fruit - skin and all!

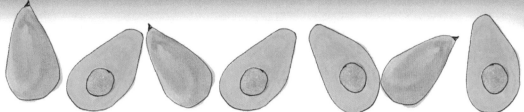

Avocado-Lime Black Bean Salsa

A quick lunch or appetizer with chips or raw veggies. Great spooned over Mexican seasoned fish or chicken.

- 1 can organic black beans drained and rinsed
- 1 avocado cut in ½ inch cubes
- 1 medium plum tomato, chopped – about ½ cup
- ¼ cup chopped red onion
- 1 Tbsp. lime juice
- 1 tsp. lime zest
- 2 Tbsp. fresh cilantro chopped
- ½ tsp. sea salt
- 1 small jalapeño pepper, finely chopped

1. Combine all ingredients in a bowl.

Goat Cheese and Basil Dip

A hearty party dip with crudités or gluten-free crackers, or as a topping on salmon cakes (see pg. 94).

- 5 oz. package fresh chèvre (goat cheese)
- 1 cup loosely packed basil leaves
- ¼ cup avocado mayonnaise
- 2 Tbsp.fresh lemon juice
- ⅓ tsp. sea salt and freshly ground black pepper
- 2 pinches of cayenne powder (optional – but adds a great zing!)
- Add a little water to create consistency for dipping

Blend all ingredients in blender or food processor.

Green Goddess Dip

One of my absolute favorite dips for raw veggies. It's also great to add a dollop on soups, savory pancakes or grilled meat.

- 1 bunch fresh cilantro
- 1 jalapeño pepper, stemmed and seeded
- 2 Tbsp. tahini – sesame seed paste
- 2 cloves garlic, peeled
- Juice of 2 limes (about 2 Tbsp.)
- ½ tsp. sea salt
- ½ large or 1 small whole avocado, flesh
- 1 Tbsp. olive oil
- ½ cup filtered water
- DARING VARIATION: Add 2 fillets of anchovies

Combine all ingredients except water in a blender or food processor, add ½ cup filtered water, and blend until smooth. Serve with raw veggies.

Nutrition Tip

Anchovies contain high amounts of omega-3 fatty acids (to help reduce inflammation). Canned in oil, they contain about 2 grams of omega-3's and also provide 29 grams of protein in each 3.5ounce serving. Anchovies are high in calcium for strong bones and teeth and a good source of iron and vitamin B-12. It doesn't take many anchovies to add that BURST of flavor to any recipe.

Serving suggestions: Mash two anchovies in a small bowl with 1 Tbsp. fresh lemon juice, 1 Tbsp. olive oil, and 2 minced garlic cloves. Add to foil wrapped green beans, chopped zucchini, or fingerling potatoes. Add a few fillets on top of any green salad for that same BURST!

Traditional Basil Pesto with Pistachios

During summer months when fresh basil is abundant, I make a double batch and freeze this pesto in ice cube trays. After frozen I take cubes out of trays and store in freezer bags in freezer. Grab a bunch of these cubes to take on your trip.

- 1 cup tightly packed fresh basil leaves
- ½ cup shelled toasted pistachios
- 2-3 cloves garlic
- 1/3 cup olive oil
- 1 Tbsp. fresh squeezed lemon juice
- ¼ tsp. sea salt
- ½ tsp. ground pepper
- 1 or more Tbsp. water

1. Add basil, pistachios, olive oil, lemon juice, garlic, salt and pepper in food processor or blender.
2. Process until well blended adding water to thin.

Nutrition Tip

Fresh herbs burst with big flavor and fragrance and a small amount can transform an ordinary meal into an extraordinary one. Herbs are rich in antioxidant phytonutrients and anti-inflammatory powers to protect our health. Fresh basil, parsley, dill and cilantro provide vitamin K, good for blood clotting and bone strength. Even small amounts of herbs are filled with minerals like iron, calcium, manganese and more. I ALWAYS bring some fresh herbs like parsley, basil or cilantro on our camping trips.

Kale Pesto

Extend the benefits of fresh herbs by adding a bitter green like kale, chard or spinach. I LOVE this pesto on zucchini noodles with sautéed red pepper, mushrooms and toasted pine nuts on top!

- 1 bunch kale leaves (about 4 cups) de-stemmed
- 3 Tbsp. fresh herbs (basil, parsley or oregano)
- 1 Tbsp. fresh mint
- ⅓ cup almonds
- 1 lemon juiced
- ⅓ cup olive oil
- 2 or more cloves garlic
- ½ tsp. sea salt & 1 tsp. fresh ground pepper

Blend all ingredients in food processor or blender. Pulse to a slightly chunky consistency adding water if necessary to thin. Serve over zucchini noodles, spaghetti squash with sautéed mushroom, or on top of eggs or sautéed veggies.

Curried Hummus

Hummus with a kick of ginger and currants.

- ¼ cup currants
- 2 cups cooked chickpeas, if you use canned – drain, rinse, and mix with a spritz of lemon juice and pinch of salt
- 2 Tbsp. water
- 2 Tbsp. fresh squeezed lemon juice
- 1 Tbsp. tahini
- 1Tbsp. olive oil
- 1 tsp. curry powder
- 1 tsp. fresh chopped ginger or ground ginger
- ½ tsp. sea salt

1. Soak the currants in water for 5 -10 minutes.
2. Combine chickpeas, water, lemon juice, tahini, olive oil, curry powder, ginger, and salt in food processor and process until smooth.
3. Transfer to a mixing bowl and add drained currants... taste.
4. Add more lemon if it needs a little zing.

Nutrition Tip

Fresh ginger root—an aromatic spice containing phytonutrients with potent anti-inflammatory properties. It's also known to soothe the stomach and relieve nausea. Soothe and heal a sore throat: Add 1–2 Tbsp. of chopped fresh ginger root to 2–3 cups water. Simmer for 10 minutes. Sip throughout your day.

Chipotle Guacamole

Who doesn't love guacamole? Heat up a can of black beans with a little Sriracha sauce and top beans with guacamole. Just add chips!

- 2 ripe Hass avocados

- 1 Tbsp. lime juice

- 2 Tbsp. cilantro (chopped)

- ¼ cup red onion (finely chopped)

- 1-2 cloves minced garlic

- ½ jalapeño, including seeds (finely chopped)

- ½ tsp. chipotle chili powder

- ¼ tsp. sea salt

1. Cut the avocado in half and the remove the pit

2. Scoop the avocados and place in a medium bowl.

3. Toss and coat with lime juice.

4. Add the salt and using a fork or potato masher, mash until a smooth consistency is achieved.

5. Fold in the remaining ingredients and mix well.

6. Taste guacamole and adjust seasoning if necessary.

Nutrition Tip

Avocados are truly a super food! They contain lots of good vitamins, minerals, phytonutrients (to reduce inflammation), healthy fats and fiber! Part of the fruit family and having the highest PROTEIN and lowest sugar content of any fruit, avocados help build lean muscle mass and burn fat.

Sriracha Mayonnaise

A spicy mayo great on fish tacos!!!

- ½ cup avocado mayonnaise
- 1 Tbsp. Sriracha Chili sauce

Nutrition Tip

Sriracha Sauce is AKA Asian ketchup, or "the World's Greatest Condiment." This lip-tingling sauce boosts the heat and umami (savory flavor) in any dish. You can make your own from scratch, but you can also pick up a bottle at any health food store.

Here's a simple way to turn Sriracha Mayonnaise into Sriracha Ranch Dressing:

½ cup avocado mayonnaise, ¼ cup full fat coconut milk, 2 Tbsp. Sriracha sauce,

1 Tbsp. lemon juice, 1 Tbsp. fresh parsley, 1 tsp. onion powder, 1 tsp. sea salt.

Toss all ingredients in a bowl and stir until smooth.

Makes a yummy dipping sauce for raw veggies too!

Easy Almond Thai Sauce

This no-brainer sauce makes your meals instantly exciting!

- ½ cup almond butter or organic peanut butter
- ½ + 1 cup filtered water (or coconut milk for a richer, sweeter sauce)
- 3 Tbsp. organic, cold-pressed sesame oil*
- 3 tsp. fish sauce or, if vegetarian, Coconut Aminos (you can add more to taste)
- 1 Tbsp. fresh minced ginger root
- 3 tsp. lime juice
- ½ bunch cilantro or basil, finely chopped
- 1 diced green onion, ends trimmed

1. Place all ingredients, except cilantro or basil and green onion in a blender or this sauce can be mixed by hand in a bowl. Mix or blend until smooth and creamy. Adjust consistency as desired.

2. Toss in half of the herbs and green onion and combine thoroughly.

3. Pour over grilled or poached chicken, fish or veggies and garnish with leftover herbs and green onion.

* Can swap organic toasted sesame oil will yield a richer flavor – but use less of the toasted – it's strong tasting.

Homemade Ketchup

Most ketchups have way too much sugar. Try this guilt-free recipe with burgers, meatballs, or foil pack roasted potatoes.

- ½ cup tomato paste

- ¼ cup apple cider vinegar

- ¼ cup apple juice

- Pinch of onion powder

- $1/3$ tsp. ground cloves

In a saucepan mix all ingredients and heat over low heat for about 5 minutes, stirring to prevent scorching. Cool and store in refrigerator for about 2 weeks.

Our son Noel and his wife Nam Fon in Alabama Hills

Yoga Stretch

Take a break from making your Secret Sauces with an invigorating Yoga Stretch!

It doesn't matter where you are or what you wear...just as long as you plan ahead and make a few secret sauces!

Side Body Stretch

Lengthen the sides of your spine and be sure to stretch both sides. Then do it again on both sides!

Salt Point State Park, CA

The YAP App

When two girlfriends get together we can talk for hours – right?

On a 2-night trip with another "camper couple", my friend Wendy and I had a lot to catch up on. The four of us hiked to a small lake in the Sierra Nevada Mountains (about 17,000 steps round trip according to my "Fit Bit").

As the guys led, Wendy and I chatted about our families, work, food – you name it - we covered it. When we arrived at a pristine lake we all jumped in to cool off. Wendy and I swam to a rock island and continued our deep conversation as the sun warmed us. And according to our men – we never shut up!

When we swam back to shore they came up with the idea of a "YAP App."

They decided we should sync our Fit Bits to a "YAP App" and count the number of words we speak as we count our steps.

What do you think?

Can we quit working and make a killing on a YAP App?

And do your lips really turn white if you talk too much?

"Humor brings insight and tolerance." –Agnes Repplier

YAP App originators

Chapter 4

4
Breakfast:
Set the Tone for Your Day

Breakfast: set the tone for your day!

Without a doubt, whether you're camping or at home— Breakfast is the most important meal of the day!

I believe food is information and the first morsels we put into our mouths bring with them a message. A healthy breakfast with plenty of protein, healthy fat and vegetables helps balance our hormones. And the best way to balance our hormones is to balance our blood sugar by eating 2-3 square meals a day.

Skipping breakfast (or any meal) or not eating enough protein or fat will signal our blood sugar to drop. When blood sugar drops, and we feel *"hangry"* our bodies start to secrete cortisol (the stress hormone) because it thinks we're going into starvation mode. Cortisol's job is to release glucose and send it to our legs and brains – so we can think quickly and *"run from the tiger."* Consuming sugary foods, especially at breakfast, prompts more cortisol production and causes the body to store more fat than needed, usually right around our midsections. Oh no!

So start your day right with:

- • At least 15–25 grams of protein (dependent on body weight and daily activities)

- • 2-3 servings of healthy fats (a serving is 1 Tbsp. of healthy oil)

- • AND lots and lots of vegetables

- • And 1 piece of fruit (optional)

Do NOT start your day with a "sugar bomb!" Keep your blood sugar stabilized by beginning your day with a protein and fat powered breakfast! Stay away from sweeteners and any foods that convert quickly to sugar—like bread, traditional pancakes, French toast or cold cereal.

Nutrition Tip:

Before breakfast and before any caffeine, drink 12-16oz. room temperature water (or hot water) with 1 Tbsp. fresh squeezed lemon juice or apple cider vinegar to alkalize your blood, build hydrochloric acid (to stimulate digestive fire) and flush your kidneys (can add a drop of stevia to sweeten). If you feel like you're run down, crave sugar or suffer from constipation, end your day with this remedy too. Take right before bed. When blood is in its natural alkaline state, joint problems ease and it creates an "unfriendly" environment for bacteria and inflammation.

Grab and Go breakfast: Quick Smoothie

When you need to hit the road early and want to avoid a bowl of cold cereal....

- One shaker cup w/stainless steel BlenderBall® or 1 quart glass jar with lid

- 1 or more cups coconut, almond or your favorite non-dairy milk. Or just use water.

- 1 scoop protein powder (Before we leave home I mix up a few protein powder packets).

To each packet or baggie I may add:

- 1 scoop protein powder (see nutrition tip below)

- 1 Tbsp. chia or hemp seeds

- 1 tsp. green powder

- 1 Tbsp. collagen powder

- 1 tsp. Ceylon cinnamon

Add everything to shaker cup, put on lid and shake, shake, shake!

Green Smoothie Breakfast Bowl

- 1 cup plain full fat goat or cow yogurt or kefir
- 1 scoop vegan or whey vanilla protein powder
- 1-2 tsp. green powder (I like Amazing Grass detox and digest powder)
- 2 Tbsp. chia, hemp or fresh ground flax seeds
- ½ cup water or nut milk
- Seasonal fruit, nuts, granola and/or coconut flakes
- Optional: stevia or maple syrup to sweeten

Nutrition Tip

ISN'T PROTEIN POWDER A PROCESSED FOOD?

Yes, but. . . today our soils are depleted and we are surrounded by so many chemical toxins, so I think it's important to supplement our diet for optimal health. I think of protein powder as a supplement. I strongly encourage using only high quality, hypoallergenic rice, pea, hemp, or chia protein powders. Most of these powders are anti-inflammatory, support detoxification, help balance blood sugar and heal your liver. If you aren't sensitive to dairy, whey protein is also a good source, but just make sure it is from grass-fed cows.

Katie's Granola Recipe

I usually don't eat a whole bowl of granola but use it more as a condiment to add texture, crunch and healthy nutrients. I sprinkle granola on my green smoothie bowl or use granola mixed with butter and a little sugar as a topping for Apple crisp or foil wrap some chopped apples (or any fruit), cinnamon, butter with gra-nola on top. As you'll notice, when I make granola I prepare a large batch and freeze half of it for later.

- 10 cups gluten free rolled oats
- 2 cups sesame seeds
- 2 cups raw unsweetened shredded coconut
- 1 tsp. sea salt

- 1 Tbsp. cinnamon

- 2-3 tsp. cardamom (optional)

- 1 tsp. nutmeg (optional)

- 1 cup coconut oil

- 2 cups applesauce or 1 cup applesauce and ½ cup maple syrup

- 1 Tbsp. vanilla

- 2 cups more or less filtered water

After Baking add:

- 2 cups pumpkin seeds

- 2 cups sunflower seeds

- 2 cups crispy almonds or walnuts – see recipe page 138

- 1 cup raisins

- 1 cup dried cranberries – unsweetened

- 1 cup large flaked raw coconut to add after baking

- 1 cup raw hemp seeds (optional)

Directions for granola:

1. Preheat oven to 300°

2. Heat coconut oil, applesauce, maple syrup if using, and vanilla in a saucepan till they form a thick liquid.

3. In a large bowl add rolled oats, shredded coconut, sesame seeds, salt and spices.

4. Add oil and applesauce "liquid" to oats along with 1 cup of the water.

5. Mix all together and add more water to make it moister. If this is not sweet enough sometimes I add a little maple syrup here – but not much!

6. Spread mixture in 2 large roasting pans and put in oven 300°. Bake for 1-1.5 hours stirring about every 20 minutes.

7. When it all turns brown – but not too brown or burnt, remove from oven and add the other nuts, seeds, dried fruit and large coconut flakes. Let cool & enjoy!

Savory Zucchini Flax Pancake

I like to make all different kinds of gluten-free pancakes when camping. Pick your favorite! Wow – pancakes have come a long way, baby!

Makes 1 pancake

- 2 tsp. avocado or coconut oil or ghee
- 1 egg
- 1-2 Tbsp. filtered water
- 2 Tbsp. Shredded zucchini, daikon radish, or carrots (swap veggies with a ripe banana for a sweeter version)
- 3 Tbsp. flax seeds, ground
- 1 packet stevia or 1 tsp. maple syrup or honey (optional)
- ¼ tsp. Ceylon cinnamon (for sweeter version pancakes)

🍄 ⁛ 🍄

1. Whisk all ingredients except cinnamon together in a bowl. Add 2 tsp. oil or ghee and heat to medium.

2. Pour mixture into pan and cook until bottom of pancake is solid enough to flip (about 3-4 minutes) If using blueberries add before flipping.

4. Flip pancake and cook about 1 more minute.

5. Serve with optimal toppings:

    a. Nut or seed butter, applesauce, sliced avocado, pesto, diced green onions, chopped cilantro, or salsa

6. For Banana Pancakes: Sprinkle with cinnamon and serve with fresh berries, plain yogurt or unsweetened applesauce.

Simple Sweet Protein Pancakes

Makes one large pancake or 2 medium

- 2 tsp. coconut oil or ghee

- 2 eggs

- 1 scoop protein powder (See tip about protein powder, page 62)

- 1 tsp. Ceylon cinnamon

- ¼ tsp. ground cloves

1. Whisk all ingredients together except oil or ghee.

2. Cook in fry pan about 2 minutes first side with 2 tsp. coconut oil or ghee.

Flip pancake and cook another 1-2 minutes.

3. Serve with berries, plain full fat yogurt, or unsweetened applesauce (or all 3!)

Nutrition Tip

BENEFITS OF FLAXSEEDS

• Always consume ground flaxseed - NOT the whole seeds, as they pass through your digestive system without being digested.

• Ground flax will go rancid so grind only a week's worth and store it in an airtight container in the refrigerator or freezer.

• Taken with any meal, ground flaxseed makes you feel full and satisfied longer – great for weight loss. Add to pancakes, smoothies, salads or soups.

• Aim for 2 to 4 tablespoons per day but work up to that gradually so that your digestive system adjusts to the high fiber content. Fiber rich foods help stabilize blood sugar and also make a very gentle, natural laxative.

Okonomiyaki

Japanese Bacon Pancakes with Shredded Cabbage

I was honored to co-lead a women's cultural retreat in Kyoto, Japan in 2018. I taught morning yoga and meditation which set the tone for our 12 day immersion. All the food was amazing but when I tasted Okonomiyaki pancakes I knew I would make them again at home. Okonomi translates to "as you like," and yaki to "grilled," which means "grilled as you like." As the name suggests, you can make these with a variety of fillings and toppings!

The foundation of okonomiyaki consists of flour, water, egg, and shredded cabbage topped with bacon. You could add a combination of onions, leeks, scallions, or grated daikon radish, zucchini or yams. They're really easy to make! These pancakes are traditionally topped with okonomiyaki sauce (found at an Asian market), mayonnaise, beni shoga (red pickled ginger), katsuobushi (bonito flakes), and aonori (seaweed flakes). But I've created my own toppings, which may be easier to find.

Makes 2, 6-inch pancakes

- 1 cup shredded green cabbage (I used my Progressive handheld mandolin slicer to cut cabbage very fine)

- 3-4 green onions - white part only, save chopped green part for topping

- ½ cup chopped onion or leek, (or grated zucchini, daikon radish or yam)

- 6 pieces of bacon, cut into thirds (you could also swap with baby shrimp)

- ½ cup ground flax seeds or ½ cup gluten-free flour (½ coconut flour and ½ arrowroot)

- 1 tsp. each of salt, pepper

- ¼ cup water

- 2 or 3 eggs

- 2 Tbsp. coconut or avocado oil (both can withstand high heat)

Toppings

- Japanese gluten-free Hoisin sauce (found at health food store)

- Avocado Mayonnaise
- Green Goddess Dip page 47
- Sliced green onions
- Kimchi
- Apple sauce with dollop of yogurt
- Sesame seeds

1. Thinly slice cabbage very fine like coleslaw

2. Thinly slice onions or leeks. Set aside.

3. In a mixing bowl, add ground flax seeds or G-F flour, salt and pepper. Whisk in water and 2 or 3 eggs. Add the veggies, into the flour mixture and stir to mix evenly.

4. In a large skillet heat 1 tbsp. of oil till almost smoking. Place half of batter in pan and flatten to make a pancake. Place ½ of bacon strips on top and cover frying pan to allow top to steam.

5. Fry for about 3-4 minutes or until golden brown. Flipping can be tricky unless you have a really large spatula to turn the whole pancake over in one swift flip. If not, try making a slice down the middle of the pancake and flip ½ at a time. Cover again for 2-3 minutes until bacon has browned (lift one edge and sneak a peek at the bacon). Repeat for the rest of the batter.

6. Serve immediately. Brush with Hoisin sauce and a healthy dose of mayo. Sprinkle green onions and add a dollop of kimchi on the side.

Homemade Hoisin Sauce

Mix together: 2 Tbsp. Tamari, 2 Tbsp. orange juice, 1 Tbsp. minced fresh ginger and 1 Tbsp. minced garlic.

Veggie Egg Nests

Feel free to play around with julienned starchy veggies — carrots, celery root, parsnip or red potatoes would work well, too.

Serves 2

- 1 medium leek (no leeks? try julienned zucchini or sliced scallions instead)
- 1 small sweet potato (I used a yam)
- 2-3 Tbsp. coconut, avocado oil or ghee
- 1 cup finely chopped kale (optional)
- ¼ tsp. salt & ¼ tsp. pepper
- ½ tsp. dried thyme
- 1 Tbsp. fresh parsley
- 4 eggs

🍄 ⁝ 🍄

1. Cut the ends off your sweet potato or yam. Using a hand-held julienne slicer (I love my Progressive mandolin) make long julienne slices of sweet potato, yam or other starchy vegetable. Thinly slice one leek avoiding the tough dark green ends.

2. In a medium-sized sauté pan add 2 Tbsp. of oil of your choice. Once hot, add leeks and julienned sweet potatoes or yam and cook for 3-5 minutes, until they are soft.

3. Remove to a bowl with the kale, thyme, and salt and pepper; toss all ingredients together.

4. Heat 1 tablespoon of oil in the same sauté pan over medium-low. Add ½ of the veggie mixture and form into a nest-type shape with a shallow hole in the middle, leaving room for two eggs.

5.   Crack 2 eggs into the middle of the nest, cover the pan with a lid, and cook for 4-8 minutes, until eggs are cooked to your preference. Repeat once more with the remaining vegetable mixture and eggs, to make a total of 2 nests.

I served this with chopped parsley, sliced oranges and 2 forkfuls of kimchi.

NUTRITION TIP

Don't be fooled by decades of misinformation about eggs. Eat them freely but make sure they are from pasture-raised chickens or are omega-3 rich eggs. (Fed flax seeds). Eggs contain cholesterol but do not cause heart disease. (Now even approved by USDA dietary guidelines). Heart disease is caused by other inflammatory factors with sugar and stress at the top of list!

Loaded Breakfast Frittata
with sweet potato crust

This is a great breakfast for a large group. Make it ahead at home or use Dutch oven over campfire.

4 servings

- 1-2 sweet potatoes or yams peeled and sliced in ¼ inch coins. Use the medium setting on a Progressive handheld mandolin slicer.

- Coconut oil spray

- ½ lb. ground turkey or savory ground pork breakfast sausage (optional)

- 1 Tbsp. + 1 tsp. coconut oil or ghee

- 1 leek sliced thin

- ½ lb. asparagus or other seasonal vegetable

- ½ cup red pepper

- 8 eggs

- 1-2 tsp. dried Italian seasoning, or herbs of choice

- Dash of garlic powder

- 1-1 ½ tsp. Celtic sea salt

- ¼ tsp. ground pepper

- ½ cup grated parmesan cheese

- Fresh chopped chives for serving

At home:

1. Preheat oven to 350°

2. Peel and slice sweet potato or yam. Spray coconut oil on bottom of 8–9" pie dish or quiche pan. Cover the whole pan and spray more coconut oil over the top of "coins".

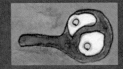

3.   Bake in oven for 20-25 minutes. Remove.

4.   While crust is baking, if using ground turkey sauté in pan with 1 tsp. coconut oil. Remove from pan. Scatter over baked sweet potato crust.

5.   Melt oil or ghee in skillet like cast iron, over medium high heat.

6.   Add sliced leek and cook for 5-10 minutes or until soft. Add red pepper and sliced asparagus

7.   In a large bowl, whisk eggs with herbs (I like 1 tsp. dill weed), garlic powder, salt and pepper.

8.   Add sautéed veggies over the ground meat, then add eggs and chives.

9.   Sprinkle parmesan cheese over top.

10. Transfer the quiche pan to the oven and bake uncovered for 20–30 minutes or until the center is puffed, the frittata is set, and a knife inserted in the center comes out clean.

Let cool for 5 minutes and slice. Serve with sautéed greens and /or raw sauerkraut.

Chorizo and Cauliflower Rice with Fried Eggs

I love this hearty breakfast recipe especially when camping. It's filling, easy and nutritious.

Serves 4

- 1 Tbsp. coconut oil
- ¾ lb. chorizo sausage
- 1 large head cauliflower cored and grated on the large hole of a box grater or hand held mandolin grater
- 3 cups baby spinach, chopped kale or chard
- 2 Tbsp. toasted pine nuts (optional)
- 4 large eggs
- Chopped parsley for garnish

1. Heat oil in large skillet over medium heat.

2. Add chorizo and cook, stirring to break up any large pieces, until almost completely browned 4–6 minutes.

3. Add cauliflower and cook, stirring occasionally for 4-5 minutes.

4. Stir in the spinach until wilted. Stir in pine nuts, if using. Serve topped with fried eggs and parsley.

NUTRITION TIP

WHY CAULIFLOWER RICE?
With the popularity of low-carb, paleo, and gluten-free lifestyles, cauliflower is so versatile and can be transformed into "rice", pizza crust, mashed "potatoes", and in baked goods. Even if you're not avoiding carbs or grains, using cauliflower is a great way to get more vegetables into your diet.

Soaked Steel Cut Oatmeal

For soaking the oats:

- 1 cup steel cut oats (not quick cooking)

- 3 cups warm water

- 1 Tbsp. of an acidic medium such as whey, plain yogurt, cultured buttermilk, kefir, lemon juice, or apple cider vinegar to breakdown phytic acid and lectins in grains. These two compounds are considered anti-nutrients for humans unless soaked. Phytic acid binds to minerals in your GI-tract so they cannot be absorbed. Lectins are proteins designed to protect plants and are abundant in grains and legumes. In humans they can cause inflammation leading to leaky gut.

For cooking the oats:

- 1 cup water
- ¼ tsp. unrefined sea salt

1. Put the steel cut oats in a glass bowl and cover with the warm water.

2. Add in your 1 Tbsp. acidic medium and stir to combine.

3. Let oats sit on counter overnight or for 8 to 12 hours.

4. Rinse oats with water. Bring 1 cup water and sea salt to boil in a pot.

5. Add in rinsed, soaked oats and simmer on low. Cook 3 to 5 minutes or until oats reach a desired consistency, stirring occasionally.

6. Serve hot with a bit of real maple syrup, ¼ tsp. Ceylon cinnamon, pastured butter, nut milk, or cream and add berries, fruit, plain yogurt or nuts.

Gluten Free Scones

I have to be honest. At first I thought these scones would be great to bake in a Dutch oven while camping. When I tried to make them "on the road" with bri-quettes on the top and bottom of my Dutch oven they turned out like little rocks. Not too appealing. But whenever I bake them at home in my oven they are such a delightful treat and satisfy that desire for a really good baked good.

My wise advice: Make these at home before hitting the road.

Personalize this recipe by adding your favorite fresh fruit ($\frac{1}{2}$ cup), dried fruit, like figs in the photo, ($\frac{1}{2}$ cup chopped and soaked in water for 15 min.), spices, nuts or seeds ($\frac{1}{2}$ cup) to the "course meal" in step 3.

Makes 12 small scones

- 2 cups gluten-free flour blend (I like Pamela's Gluten-Free flour blend. Can substitute ¼ cup almond flour for added protein and fiber)

- 1 Tbsp. non-aluminum double acting baking powder

- ½ tsp. xanthan gum (if sensitive to processed xanthan gum swap for ½ tsp. chia seeds or psyllium husk fiber)

- ¼ tsp. sea salt

- ½ cup cold unsalted pasture raised butter

- 2 large eggs

- 1 Tbsp. honey

- $\frac{1}{3}$ coconut cream, half and half, or cream (I actually didn't even use this because my dough felt too moist)

- Egg glaze (1 egg yolk mixed with 2 Tbs. cream or nut milk for brushing)

- Coconut sugar (optional for dusting)

1. Heat oven to 350°

2. In a large mixing bowl, whisk together flour blend, baking powder, xanthan gum (or chia or psyllium husk fiber) and salt.

3. Toss butter into dry ingredients. Using fingers or a pastry cutter, work butter in to dry ingredients to create a coarse meal (this is where you would add optional fresh or dried fruit, spices, nuts or seeds)

4. Make a well in the dry ingredients and break eggs into well. Pour honey and start with a small amount of cream and mix together to form a slightly sticky dough. If needed add more cream, 1 Tbsp. at a time until dough comes together.

5. Dump dough onto lightly floured cutting board or parchment paper. Shape into 2 round flat cakes about 1 inch thick and cut each cake into 6 equal triangles. (for larger scones, pat dough into one round cake about 8 inch wide and 3/4 inch thick. Cut into 8 equal triangles). Brush each scone with egg glaze or just plain cream and sprinkle with optional coconut sugar and cinnamon.

6. Arrange scones on parchment paper covered cookie sheet. Bake for 18–20 minutes (depending on thickness and size)

7. Remove from oven and let cool before eating.

Before Breakfast Yoga Postures

Before making breakfast, take time for a few simple stretches to get your Prana (life force energy) moving.

(For more detailed instructions refer to specific page number.)

Down Dog

Warm up your spine practicing with hands on picnic table bench. (See detailed instructions, page 198.)

Plank Pose

Open the front body by moving into Up Dog or Plank Pose. (page 198)

Lunge

Open hip flexors and quadriceps with a lunge. With one foot on the bench, hop other foot back so your heel is off the ground. Hands on table or in your pockets if it's cold. (page 199)

Rhyolite, Nevada

On the Road Again

We're on the road again,
Goin' places where we've never been.
Making love again with my best friend, it's true...
Oh...we just can't wait to get on the road again.

(SUNG TO WILLIE NELSON'S ON THE ROAD AGAIN)

Bill and I have been married for over 43 years. We're in that rare club of partners in truly long-term relationships. It seems there aren't too many members of this organization, and one of the ways we keep our "spark" alive is to shake things up.

When we first hit the road without kids, we almost didn't know how to handle so much freedom. It didn't take us long to recognize that our playful, child-like selves were coming back out. We began to see and experience the person we had fallen in love with back in 1975.

Without the responsibility of parenting, we had each other's complete attention.

I witnessed Bill in his "happy place," as he rediscovered his spirit for adventure in the great outdoors.

As a self–employed, hardworking landscape contractor with kids, taking time off for Bill had usually meant family camping or visiting grandparents. Sometimes those vacations were more draining than our everyday jobs.

Now, we had earned our freedom. Shortly after our second son left for college, we had saved enough income to purchase the "Tiger."

And that's when our renewed LOVE story began.

I witnessed my man back in his power. He seemed to stand taller and carry the confidence of a wild animal. I loved when he would start planning our next adventure shortly after returning home from the last one.

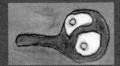

I was attracted all over again to Bill's beautiful sense of stewardship for the land and his deep desire to make sure I was feeling safe and secure in the backcountry. I was in awe of the joy he found in practicing "How to survive in the wilderness" and I even found pleasure in his rough and stubbly wilderness beard.

Spending time in the wilderness brought about my own transformation. Life became an adventure with excitement and anticipation for our special get-a-ways. I put more effort into planning delicious, whole food meals and started to record successful recipes. I brought along art supplies and started to draw and paint on the spacious days we spent in one place. I began to sleep more soundly, and my menopausal mood swings were more manageable. And I felt healthy, fit and sensual again from all the hiking and outdoor living with my sweetheart.

Throughout our marriage we've experienced good and bad times. I think the most important message I can share with readers is to keep shaking things up. Practicing basic survival and communication skills in the wilderness, having adventures and seeing new sights, is one great way to maintain a juicy relationship. I encourage you to seek your favorite ways to keep your special connections ALIVE!

Chapter 5

5
Lunch:
at the Rest Stop, Picnic or Campsite

Lunch at the Rest Stop

When we're on the road we usually eat lunch at a rest stop, or once settled into a camp spot we may pack lunch in our backpacks for a hike or other adventure. Here are a few of my favorites:

• Finger food is easiest (cheese, crackers, salsa, sliced turkey, avocados, raw celery, carrots or jicama with almond butter or hummus, fruit and don't forget the dark chocolate!)

• Leftover dinner can be a treat if you can heat it up.

• If we're near our camp kitchen I prepare salads with a hearty dose of protein and fat!

A typical packed lunch for 2, complete with homemade strawberry rhubarb crisp for dessert.

Salad Dressings & Salads

Basic Salad Dressing

(1-2 Tbsp/salad)

- Start with oil and lemon juice or vinegar at ratio of 3:1 oil : vinegar or juice

- Oil: extra virgin olive, flax, walnut, or avocado

- Lemon or lime juice, apple cider vinegar, balsamic or wine vinegar

- **Optional**: Dijon mustard – ½-1 tsp, seasonings including salt, fresh ground pepper, fresh or dried herbs, or avocado or tahini to make dressing creamy.

Creamy Garlic Dressing

makes 10 servings, about 2 Tbsp. each

- ½ cup extra virgin olive oil

- ¼ cup apple cider vinegar

- 3 cloves garlic (crushed)

- 1-2 Tbsp. fresh lemon juice

- 2 Tbsp. chopped fresh parsley

- 1 tsp. Himalayan salt

- ½ tsp. Dijon mustard

- 1-2 tsp. raw honey or pure maple syrup

Place oil, vinegar, garlic, lemon juice, parsley, salt, mustard and honey in a blender or food processor; blend till smooth. Stir before serving and refrigerate leftover dressing.

Mustard Lemongrette Dressing

- ¼ cup virgin olive oil

- 2 ½ Tbsp. lemon juice

- 2 Tbsp. minced red onions (optional)

- 1 Tbsp. Light miso

- 1 Tbsp. Dijon mustard

- 1 tsp. sweetener of your choice (I like maple syrup, or just a few drops of stevia)

- ½ tsp. sea salt

Mix all together with wire whisk in a bowl.

Apple Beet Salad

You must make this salad! Not only does it make your taste buds sing, but beets, green apples and lemons are great for liver and gall bladder support. I shared this recipe with my Thai daughter-in-law and she added a South East Asian influence. See options below.

- 1 organic red beet

- 1 organic apple

- Juice of ½ lemon

- *Optional* – 1-2 tsp. minced fresh ginger, 2 Tbsp. chopped cilantro or fresh mint and replace lemon juice with fresh lime juice! Enjoy!

A Lovely Kale Salad

- 2 big bunches organic kale, de-stemmed
- 1 Tbsp. lemon juice
- 1 Tbsp. olive oil
- 1 tsp. sea salt
- 2 cups sunflower sprouts (optional)
- 1 avocado cubed
- ½ cup chopped walnuts or crispy pumpkin seeds
- 2 Tbsp. capers
- 2–3 peeled & sectioned mandarin oranges, 6-8 large strawberries halved, or 1 or 2 sliced peaches or nectarines

1. Slice kale leaves into thin strips (chiffonade), transfer to a large mixing bowl, drizzle with lemon juice and olive oil, and sprinkle on sea salt. Gently massage for 3–5 minutes, until they start to soften and turn dark green.

2. Add capers, sprouts, and walnuts or pumpkin seeds and toss with about ½ cup of tahini dressing (recipe below). Place sliced fruit and avocado chunks around edge of bowl.

Tahini dressing - (*makes 3/4 cup*)

- 1 clove garlic
- ¼ cup tahini
- ¼ cup flax, hemp or olive oil
- 2 Tbsp. gluten-free tamari or coconut aminos
- 2 Tbsp. fresh lemon juice
- ¼ cup water or more as needed for desired consistency

Place all ingredients, except water in blender. Blend until well mixed. Add water 1 tbsp. at a time until desired consistency is achieved. It gets thicker in the fridge.

Jicama Lime Coleslaw

One of my favorite recipes for coleslaw with 2 dressing variations.

- 1 small jicama (about 1 ¼ lbs.), peeled and julienned
- ¼ head red cabbage, cored and very thinly sliced
- ¼ head green cabbage cored and sliced thin
- ¼ cup chopped fresh cilantro or basil
- 2 Tbsp. chopped fresh mint
- ⅓ cup chopped roasted almonds – add right before serving

Dressing #1 (more complex but extremely tasty)

- 1 Tbsp. sesame oil
- ½-1 tsp. diced and seeded jalapeño pepper
- 3 tablespoons unseasoned rice vinegar
- 2 tablespoons fresh lime juice
- 2 Tbsp. coconut aminos or gluten free tamari
- 1 Tbsp. minced fresh ginger root (***secret ingredient!***)
- Pinch of sea salt
- 1 Tbsp. maple syrup

Whisk all together and pour over veggies. Serve with chopped toasted almonds.

Dressing #2 (very simple!)

- ⅓ cup avocado mayonnaise

- 1 tsp. sriracha sauce (*secret ingredient!*))

- 1-2 Tbsp. lime juice

Stir all together and mix with veggies.

How to Make It

1.   At home: put cut vegetables and herbs in a large re-sealable plastic bag. Keep chilled up to 2 days.

2.   At home: combine oil, vinegar, lime juice, coconut aminos, salt, maple syrup, in a small container. Keep chilled up to 2 days.

3.   At campsite: add dressing to vegetables, shake to combine well, and let sit 15 minutes, stirring 2 or 3 times. Serve garnished with cilantro, or along-side meatballs (see recipe, pg. 114) .

Asian Chicken Slaw

Don't let this long list of ingredients scare you – the end result is totally worth the effort. You can make the dressing at home or at camp. I used my handheld Progressive mandolin julienne slicer and it was so easy to make. I set the slicer on #2 setting.

- 2 cups diced, cooked chicken
- 1 small green cabbage, shredded
- 1 small red cabbage, shredded
- 2 carrots, shredded & peeled
- ½ cup green onions white and green parts sliced diagonally
- 2 cloves garlic, minced
- 1 Tbsp. ginger, grated – don't forget this tasty ingredient!
- ¼ cup almond butter
- 2 Tbsp. raw honey
- 2 Tbsp. coconut aminos or gluten-free tamari sauce
- 2 Tbsp. coconut vinegar or apple cider vinegar
- ½ lime, juiced
- ¼ cup avocado or light flavored olive oil
- 1 tsp. sesame oil
- ½-1 tsp. sriracha
- Optional: ¼ cup chopped fresh basil or cilantro
- Pinch of salt
- Optional toppings
- ¼ cup chopped almonds or cashews
- 2 Tbsp. sesame seeds

Instructions

1. Shred cabbage and carrots. Add with chopped green onions and chicken to a large bowl.

2. In a medium sized bowl, combine almond butter, oils, honey, garlic, ginger, limejuice, salt and sriracha (taste, using ½ tsp. and add more if you want more spice). Whisk.

3. Pour dressing over the shredded cabbage/carrots and toss.

4. Top off with fresh herbs & chopped almonds, cashews or sesame seeds, if desired.

My Favorite Kimchi Recipe

Prepare at home before leaving on your trip. I try to eat this traditional Korean kimchi with just about everything savory. If you don't like the spicy heat, leave out the Korean chili flakes.

- 1 (2.5 lb.) green cabbage cut into 2 x 1inch pieces

- 2 Tbsp. sea salt plus 2 tsp.

- 6 scallions, trimmed and cut in to 2 inch pieces, greens and whites separated

- 1 (2 inch) piece of ginger peeled and thinly sliced. (If ginger is organic I just scrub it well and forget peeling it)

- 1 medium Asian pear or apple cored and roughly chopped

- 2 tsp. fish sauce

- 2 Tbsp. Korean chili flakes if making spicy kimchi

- 1 large carrot, cut in to thin ¼ inch coins

- 1 small red pepper cut into matchsticks or julienned

- 3 cloves garlic, peeled thinly sliced

- 2 tsp. black sesame seeds (Optional)

1.   In a large bowl toss cut cabbage with 2 Tbsp. sea salt – Important first step and saves time massaging cabbage.

2.   Set aside to create a brine for 1 hour

3.   Transfer cabbage to a colander and rinse with cool water. Leave cabbage in colander to drain.

4.   Put scallion whites, ginger, Asian pear, fish sauce and 2 tsp. of salt in a blender or food processor. Blend until smooth.

5.   If making spicy kimchi, transfer paste to bowl and stir in Korean chili flakes.

6. In large bowl, combine drained cabbage with scallion greens, carrot, red bell pepper and garlic.

7. Pour paste in bowl and mix well with other ingredients. You may want to use gloves if making spicy kimchi. It's hot!

8. Pack kimchi tightly into 2-quart jars, leaving 1 inch of space at top.

9. Cover container tightly with a plastic lid.

10. Leave them on a rimmed baking sheet or tray for 3-7 days, depending on how tangy you like your kimchi. Taste it!

11. If desired, top with sesame seeds before eating.

Benefits of consuming fermented veggies with meals

Cultured or fermented veggies are naturally packed with digestive enzymes and probiotics, which support the health of your digestive system. Eating cultured foods regularly can help reduce sugar cravings and help the body break down healthy fats.

Turkey / Chicken Patties

(I like to double this recipe using 1 lb. ground turkey and 1 lb. chicken.) Great for breakfast, lunch or dinner with sautéed veggies.

- 1 lb. ground organic chicken or turkey
- 1 onion, finely diced
- 1 Tbsp. extra virgin olive oil
- 1 tsp. dried or fresh thyme
- 2 tsp. dried or fresh oregano, or basil
- 2 tsp. dried sage
- 1 tsp. crushed fennel seeds (optional)
- $\frac{1}{8}$ tsp. red pepper flakes (optional)
- 2 cloves garlic, minced, or 1 tsp. garlic powder
- 2 tsp. dulse, soaked (seaweed - optional)
- ½ -1 tsp. sea salt
- ¼ tsp. ground pepper
- Add ¼ cup gluten-free oats or 1-2 Tbsp. coconut flour if patties feel too moist.
- *Optional Asian spiced patties*: Instead of thyme, oregano, sage and fennel seeds, Use 2 Tbsp. minced fresh ginger, 2-4 cloves garlic minced, ¼ tsp. red pepper flakes).
- *Optional Southwest Turkey Patties*: Replace herbs with ½ (7-oz) can chipotle peppers in adobo sauce, minced, 3 Tbsp. chopped fresh cilantro & ½ tsp chili powder.

1. Mix the ground meat, diced onions, olive oil, and spices in a large bowl, or

in a food processor. Add enough olive oil to help achieve adequate moistness, since ground poultry can be dry.

2. Divide mixture into 6 equal parts and roll each part into a ball and flatten into a patty. The patties will shrink when cooked, so make them about 25% larger than you want the cooked patties to be.

3. To freeze for later use: Put each patty between layers of waxed paper or parchment paper or into its own bag, and then put 2 or 3 into a ziplock bag. Try to eliminate air in the bag to prevent freezer burn.

4. To cook: Melt some ghee, or coconut oil in a skillet with a lid to prevent burning at medium heat. Sauté patties for about 7 minutes on each side (longer if frozen) until golden brown. Serve over cooked leafy green vegetables with mushrooms, fried egg and fermented sauerkraut. Could also serve with salsa and avocado, or homemade ketchup page 54.

Salmon Cakes

I always bring a can or two of wild caught salmon to prepare these delicious salmon burgers with a salad. Frying them in lots of coconut oil is key to making them crispy. Great for brain, heart and metabolic function.

Makes 2-3 servings

- ¼ red onion, finely chopped
- 1 large clove garlic
- 1-2 Tbsp. chopped fresh chives (set 1 tsp. aside for garnish)
- 1 Tbsp. Dijon mustard
- 1 egg
- Sea salt & pepper to taste
- 6 oz. cooked wild salmon, mashed up (I use canned wild salmon)
- 1 Tbsp. coconut flour (crushed gluten free crackers work too)
- ¼ cup coconut oil
- Juice & zest of ½ lemon for garnish
- **Optional:** serve with dollop of crème fraiche mixed with a little horseradish, or goat cheese basil dip, page 46

🍄 ⋰⋱ 🍄

1. Pre-heat a small cast iron skillet w/ coconut oil melted about ¼" deep.

2. Combine onion, garlic, chives, mustard, sea salt, pepper and egg in a small mixing bowl to combine. Add coconut flour here if desired for an extra binding agent.

3. Add in salmon and mix together until the salmon is well incorporated.

4.   When the pan and oil are hot, form the mixture into approximately 2 patties.

5.   Cook the patties thoroughly until well browned on one side before attempting to flip them. If you try to flip them too early they may break. Brown the second side. Each side will take several minutes to brown.

6.   Remove the salmon cakes from the pan and serve warm. Garnish with extra chives, onions and lemon juice and zest to taste. I served this over salad greens with mango kumquat salsa (page 44) and a dollop of green goddess dip, page 47.

Egg, Potato, Chicken or Salmon Salad

Use one or a combination of these players in your next hearty salad.

Serves 2

- 3-4 peeled hard boiled eggs, or 12 oz. can wild caught salmon (rinsed and drained), 8 oz. cooked chicken, or 1 lb. potatoes (quartered and boiled all dente)
- 2 celery stalks, slice thin or chopped
- 2 chopped scallions, or ¼ cup chopped red onion, or 1 tsp. onion flakes
- ½ chopped cucumber
- 2-3 raw garlic (optional)
- Pinch red pepper flakes (optional)
- Chopped Romaine lettuce or baby arugula

Dressing

- 2 Tbsp. avocado mayonnaise
- 1 tsp. Dijon mustard
- ½ lime juiced
- Salt and pepper to tastes.

Mix all ingredients together and enjoy a yummy lunch!

Eggamole

A delightful combination of hard cooked eggs and mashed avocado.

Makes about 2¼ cups

In a large bowl, gently mix 6 chopped hardboiled eggs, 1 avocado, and $\frac{1}{3}$ cup plain Greek yogurt until well combined. Mix in 1 medium tomato, chopped, and 2 Tbsp. finely chopped red onion (optional). Serve with raw veggies or gluten-free crackers.

Yoga with a View

Balancing a gorgeous view with the joy of simply feeling ALIVE!

Tree Pose

South Rim Grande Canyon

Tend and Befriend

Stress or a threat to survival can bring about different behaviors in men and women. The primary male response to stress is "fight or flight."

The primary female response is often called "tend and befriend".

This behavior refers to protecting offspring (tending) and/or making contact with other women in order to ensure survival (befriending). From an evolutionary standpoint, women evolved as caregivers. If a woman were to fight and lose, she would either have to leave her child behind (an unacceptable solution) —or flee, something far more difficult while carrying a child—also probably a loss.

Imagine this scene at a dump station at the north rim of the Grand Canyon campground: we meet a couple, about our age, traveling in a cool looking travel trailer we'd never seen before-an easy topic to start a conversation while taking care of our camper basic needs.

We discovered this couple had just met a few months ago and were taking their first trip together in HER trailer. While our guys were discussing hookups and generators my "new" girlfriend asked if I wanted to see the inside of HER camper.

It's always intriguing to see how other couples live on the road. Their "Forest River Trailer" had a well-designed and colorful interior. I admired the beautiful pillows and curtains that adorned the living space and when parked, the side-walls popped out to create more spaciousness. After about a minute on the tour, though, she began bashing her new boyfriend.

" I'm about to go crazy! This guy tries to control all that we do and thinks he knows everything about MY trailer!"

"I feel stuck out here with a man who doesn't eat the same way I do"

"I don't know if I can stand this another week before we get home!"

Oh my! This woman was not a happy camper!

I was surprised that she totally dumped on me, but being female, I didn't try to "fix her". I simply listened and asked a few questions like how well did she know this guy before they planned the trip. I was hoping to make more sense out of her distressing tale and allow her to just express her feelings.

Of course I didn't have the answer or time to hangout and keep listening.

My thought was if her ears could HEAR what her heart FELT, perhaps she could reconfigure her reaction and find a sense of peace to survive her situation.

Our total visit at the dump station lasted about 10 potent minutes. As we drove away I felt a kindred connection with this woman, who befriended me with her true feelings. I sent them both a blessing of peace and understanding and hoped she felt safe and confident to share her frustrations with her partner. I also felt a deeper sense of appreciation for my Bill.

Except at mating time, Elk honor the company of their own gender. This message teaches us to seek connection with brotherhood and sisterhood, to air feelings in safety and overcome potential competition and jealousy of our same sex.

Elk Medicine-our Spirit Guide

Chapter 6

6
Dinner:
on the Grill or
in Your Tiny Kitchen

Bill's Barbeque Tips On the Road

Barbequing just about anything really depends on whether you can safely make a campfire. If it's windy or lightly raining we may opt to grill on our portable small propane barbeque in a secluded spot right next to the camper. When weather conditions are more severe, we sauté food inside our tiny kitchen.

1. **Wood vs. briquettes** - Bill prefers to use coals or briquettes for more controlled grilling. He gets the campfire going with wood and allows it to burn down. If using hard wood (*oak, Doug fir, Madrone or fruit tree wood*) that burns hot, you may not need to add briquettes. If wood is funky he adds a few briquettes and waits till the flames burn down to a nice bed of coals.

2. **Testing coals** – Place the backside of your hand about 6 inches from the coals. If coals are ready you'll want to remove your hand right away. If hand can remain there for a while, let coals heat up longer.

Once coals are hot, you have a window of about 30 minutes to cook your food. Remember, though, you can always add more briquettes to keep the fire hot longer.

3. **Foil wrapped food** – Place packets on the side of coals – do not set on top of grill or directly on top of coals. You want these packets to cook slow and steady. See more foil packet cooking guidelines on page 122.

4. **Campfire ring grills vs. portable grilling rack** - the grills that attach to campground fire rings are usually too large or too high from coals. Bill likes to use a portable grill with folding legs that he sets right above the coals. NO Campfire? No problem. We use a small stainless steel propane barbeque that stores nicely in our camper.

5. **Preparing meat or produce for grilling** - keep marinade simple or you'll have flames from fancy marinades that contain sugar. Toss with marinades or sauces after grilling.

    a. Allow meat to come to room temperature

    b. Marinade for FISH:

        i.   1 part lemon juice

        ii. 1 part olive oil (when using propane grill use very little olive oil as it tends to create flames)

        iii. Sea salt & pepper or Gomasio salt with sesame seeds

        iv. Chopped garlic (optional)

    c. Marinade for meat or poultry

        i.   Same marinade as above except omit the lemon juice

6. **Use a thermometer!** It's the best way to test for meat "doneness". They work wonders every time! Optimal and safe temperatures for medium:

    a. Beef, lamb, pork 145°

    b. Poultry 165°

7. **Grilling corn on the cob** – Soak whole corn with husks in salt water for at least an hour or more. Leave husks on and grill till corn starts to steam and outer husk leaves start to burn.

8. **Grilling skewers** - Basting is very important when grilling skewers because they dry out quickly. Baste with simple marinade recipe above.

Dinner Recipes

Grilled Portabella Mushrooms with Pesto

This is one of the easiest ways to cook mushrooms on a grill or roast in an oven, if you happen to have one on the road. Serves 2

- 2 large portabella mushrooms
- 1/3 cup pesto (see recipe page 48)
- A little olive oil, salt and pepper

1. Slice stems off mushrooms.
2. Brush with olive oil. Season with salt and pepper.
3. Turn upside down and spread pesto on inside of mushrooms.
4. Grill slowly for about 4-5 minutes or until pesto begins to bubble.
5. ENJOY with your favorite grilled meats.

Dinner Menu Idea

1. Grilled New York or Rib eye Steak
2. Grilled portabella mushrooms with pesto
3. Foil packet fingerling potatoes with parsley
4. Foil packet green beans and corn
5. Chocolate coconut fondue with chunks of melon and cherries

Grilled Steak with Cilantro-Lime Vinaigrette

A classic Southeast Asian combination of aromatic ingredients that maintain fresh-ness and individual flavors when combined just before serving!

- 2 lbs. sirloin, New York or Rib eye steak (from grass-fed cows of course)

- ¼ cup olive oil

- Sea salt and fresh ground pepper

Rub steaks with olive oil, salt and pepper and mix well.

While grill heats up, prepare the vinaigrette in medium size bowl

- ½ cup roughly chopped fresh cilantro leaves (or basil)

- ¼ cup olive oil

- ¼ cup lime juice (from 2 limes)

- 1 Tbsp. minced garlic

- 1 Tbsp. chili powder or 1 tsp. chili flakes

- 1 Tbsp. mince fresh ginger (optional)

- Sea salt and fresh ground pepper

1. Grill steaks directly over coals. Cook until done to your liking – about 4 – 6 minutes per side for medium rare. (Remember they will continue to cook after being taken off grill). Check for doneness using a meat thermometer (145° for Beef) Remove from grill and let rest for 5 minutes.

2. Thinly slice steaks against the grain and place in bowl with the marinade

Serving suggestions:

- Serve steak slices on top of hearty green salad with vinaigrette.

- Serve with jicama lime coleslaw (page 86) and roasted foil packets of potatoes and fennel (page 124).

- Serve with mushroom and lemongrass packets (page 129) and spicy sweet potato packets (page 126).

Chicken, Pork or Beef Skewers

- 1.5 lbs. boneless chicken breasts, pork (tenderloin's my favorite), or beef (sirloin works well)

- 1 large red pepper or summer squash cut in 1 ½ inch chunks

- 1 large red onion cut in 1 ½ inch chunks

Marinade – *mix together*

- ½ cup gluten free tamari

- ¼ cup rice vinegar

- 1 Tbsp. ginger root grated (I like lots of ginger!)

- 3 cloves garlic crushed

- 2 Tbsp. sesame oil

- ½ tsp. chili flakes

- ½ tsp. 5 spice powder (Optional)

- Grilled half peaches (in summer) or apples (in winter) add an exquisite flavor burst to this meal

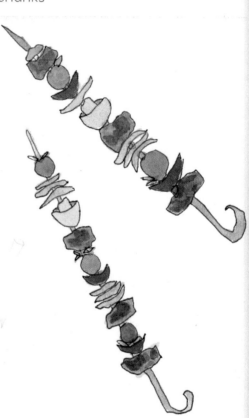

1. Cut chicken breasts or other protein into 1 ½ inch chunks and marinate for 30-60 minutes.

2. Thread onions, peppers and meat on skewers alternating them. Repeat until you've used up all veggies and protein.

3. Grill skewers on charcoal, gas or wood fired grill.

4. Turn often until veggies and protein have some charring on them (10–20 minutes).

5. Near the end of grilling brush again with extra marinade.

6. Serve over bed of sautéed greens, cauliflower rice or green salad with sliced pears and creamy garlic dressing..

Gilled Fish and Corn Tacos

Incredibly delicious, very colorful and everybody loves these! Make extra!!!! Don't forget the salsa!

- ½ cup olive or avocado oil mayonnaise

- 1 Tbsp. Sriracha sauce

- 3 Tbsp. avocado or olive oil

- 2 cloves garlic

- 1 tsp. each dried oregano and ground cumin

- ½ tsp. sea salt

- ¼ tsp. cayenne and freshly ground pepper

- 1 lb. skinned Pacific rockfish fillets, steelhead trout or wild caught salmon

- 8 corn tortillas (**or use Siete brand casava tortillas if you're grain sensitive**)

- 2 ears of corn, husks and silk removed

- 1 avocado

- 1 cup finely shredded red cabbage

- ½ cup cilantro

1. Heat grill to high (450°–550°)

2. In a small bowl combine mayonnaise and Sriracha sauce; chill.

3. In a glass pie pan combine oil, garlic oregano, cumin, salt, cayenne, and pepper. Turn fish in seasoned oil.

4. Seal tortillas in foil

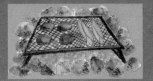

5. Grill corn, covered and turning a few times until lightly roasted, 8–10 minutes.

6. Five minutes after putting corn on grill, set large cast iron pan on cooking grate. After a few minutes, put fish in hot skillet and tortilla packet on grate.

7. Cook turning fish and tortillas once, until fish is translucent in center (3-5 minutes). And tortillas are hot.

8. Cut kernels off corn in slabs. Spread tortillas with Sriracha mayo and put rest in a small dish. Fill tortillas with chunks of fish, avocado, cabbage, cilantro and corn.

9. Serve with Peach Kumquat Salsa (page 44) and more Sriracha mayo on the side.

Grilled Za'atar Chicken with Lemon

One of our Iranian friends gave us a bottle of Green Za'atar seasoning and I never knew how to use it . . . until I discovered this incredibly simple recipe in Sunset Magazine. Za'atar contains a lovely combination of Mediterranean herbs and spices including thyme, oregano, sesame seeds, salt and sumac. **Sumac** *is the secret ingredient that comes from deep red berries of the sumac bush (native to the Middle east). The berries are dried and ground into a powder adding a tangy lemony flavor to any dish. Try it on eggs, potatoes or fish. Serves 4.*

- ¼ cup olive oil

- 2 Tbsp. Zaatar (*Find in the spice aisle of well-stocked grocery stores or at worldspice.com*)

- 2 Tbsp. lemon juice

- 1 tsp. lemon zest

- 1 tsp. minced garlic

- ¼ tsp. salt

- ¼ teaspoon pepper

- 4 chicken thighs with bone and skin (6 to 8 oz. each)

- 1 lemon, cut into 4 wedges

1. Whisk together oil, Zaatar, lemon juice, zest, garlic, salt, and pepper in a large bowl. Add chicken and turn to coat.

2. Heat grill to medium (350° to 450°). Grill chicken, skin side down, until browned, 5 to 8 minutes; watch for flare-ups and move chicken to a cooler spot if needed. Turn chicken and grill until cooked through, about 4 minutes.

3. Grill lemon wedges in last few minutes, turning once, just until grill marks appear. Serve with chicken.

Serving suggestion: Serve with large green salad with Mustard Lemon-grette Dressing (page 84) Or with zucchini noodles (*AKA zoodles* - julienned on your Progressive handheld mandolin and basil kale pesto (page 49).

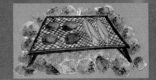

Bison Burgers

I think Bison meat is tastier than beef and richer in flavor. Most bison is grass fed and pasture raised and is lower in saturated fat than regular cow beef. Bison is a great source of basic nutrients: zinc, niacin, iron, vitamin B6 and selenium.

- 1 lb. Ground Bison meat
- ¼ chopped onion – red or yellow
- ½ tsp. sea salt
- ½ tsp. pepper
- Optional: 1–2 minced garlic, 1 tsp. Za'atar seasoning or 1 tsp. oregano or thyme

1. Mix meat with other ingredients in large bowl.
2. Shape into four 1/2-inch-thick patties.
3. Grill burgers on medium to high heat (350° to 450°). Grill for about 2-3 minutes per side for medium rare.
4. Or if sautéing heat 1 Tbsp. avocado or coconut oil in heavy large skillet over high heat. Sprinkle burgers with salt and pepper; add to skillet. Cook until well browned, about 2 minutes per side for medium-rare.

Serving suggestion: Serve with large green salad and berry ginger chutney (page 43) over greens and burger. Can also serve smothered with sautéed onions with homemade ketchup (page 54) and mustard.

Nutrition Tip:

Are Bison and buffalo the same animal?
NO, the American Bison is native to North and South America and Europe, while buffalo reside in Africa and Asia.

Vegetarian or Meaty Chili

I never had chili with so many vegetables and it's fantastic! You can make this in a Dutch oven or on your stovetop. Don't forget to bring a big enough pot! Serves 4.

- 1 lb. Free-range ground turkey, beef or pork or 1 ½ cups adzuki beans for vegetarians

- 2 Tbsp. extra virgin olive oil

- 1 medium red onion diced

- 4 garlic cloves, minced

- 2 tsp. each ground cumin, chili powder, paprika

- ½ tsp. sea salt

- Dash of ground pepper

- 12 shiitake mushrooms

- 2 cups chopped cauliflower

- 2-4 medium tomatoes (optional) or 1 can chopped tomatoes

- 2 carrots chopped

- 1 can red, black or pinto beans

- 4 cups chicken broth

- 1 cup water if needed

- ½ cup chopped parsley

- *Optional* – grated parmesan, feta or goat cheese

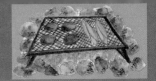

1. In a large soup pot heat olive oil on low to medium heat, sauté onion and garlic until soft – about 2-3 minutes. Add cumin, chili powder, paprika, salt and pepper.

2. Add turkey and brown for about 5-7 minutes.

3. Add mushrooms, cauliflower, carrots, tomatoes, beans, broth and additional water if needed. Cook for 8–10 minutes more, stirring consistently. Season to taste.

4. Serve and sprinkle with chopped parsley and cheese.

Turkey, Beef or Pork Meatballs

Whenever I make meatballs I always prepare extra ones to snack on the next day. At home I usually bake them in the oven on parchment paper but when camping I sauté them in a cast iron skillet on the grill or cook stove. Or if you're adventurous try threading them on a skewer stick and cook on grill over campfire. And there are plenty of variations!!! Here are two of my favorites:

Spicy Turkey Meatballs

I substituted ground chicken and needed to add 2 Tbsp. ground flax seeds to thicken the meatballs.

- 1 lb. ground turkey meat
- ¼ yellow or white onion, finely diced
- 3 large cloves of garlic, grated or finely diced
- 2 Tbsp. chopped fresh cilantro
- 1 tsp. cumin powder
- 1 tsp. onion powder
- $\frac{1}{3}$ tsp. sea salt
- 1 Tbsp. tomato paste
- 2 Tbsp. hot sauce or 1 Tbsp. Sriracha sauce
- A pinch of pepper
- 1 egg (can be omitted) or add 1 Tbsp. fresh ground flax seed
- ***For cooking***: dash of olive oil and more hot sauce
- ***To serve***: extra hot sauce, lime wedges and coriander (optional)

1. In a mixing bowl, add all ingredients except Sriracha sauce and mix everything really well so the flavors and ingredients are well incorporated (I used my hands to do this).

2. Roll the meat mixture into medium-size balls (a little smaller than a ping pong ball).

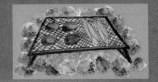

3. Sauté the meatballs over medium heat on grill or cook stove. When almost cooked drizzle Sriracha sauce on them.

4. Remove from skillet and serve with extra hot sauce and some lime wedges or add to any vegetable stir-fry.

Serving Suggestion: Serve meatballs over zucchini noodles with Basil Pesto with Pistachios (page 48) and roasted pine nuts.

Thai Meatballs - *So easy and so tasty!!!!*

- 1 lb. ground beef, lamb, turkey or pork
- 2 Tbsp. red curry paste
- $\frac{1}{3}$ cup coconut cream (use solid part of cream on top from can)
- 2 eggs
- 1-2 Tbsp. ground flax seeds or 1-2 Tbsp. coconut flour to thicken
- ¼ cup chopped fresh cilantro
- ¼ cup chopped fresh mint
- 1 tsp. chili flakes
- 1 Tbsp. coconut oil

In a large bowl mix all ingredients. Form into 16 little meatballs. You can either sauté these babies in a skillet with 1 Tbsp. coconut oil or thread them on a skewer and cook on grill. Cook until they are just pink inside, about 4-5 minutes.

Serving suggestion: Serve with cucumber, tomato chutney below..

Cucumber, Tomato and Mint Chutney

- 2 medium cucumbers
- 2 Roma tomatoes
- ½ cup plain full fat plain yogurt
- 1 Tbsp. olive oil
- 1 tsp. minced garlic
- 2 Tbsp. chopped fresh mint
- 2 Tbsp. lemon juice

1. Peel cucumber (***if not organic***), cut them in half lengthwise, and then scoop out seeds with a spoon (optional). Cut tomatoes in half and mince both cucumbers and tomatoes. Combine all ingredients in a small salad bowl and toss.

Campfire Yoga Stretch

Campfire's ready!

While waiting for dinner I practice a few yoga stretches.

Boondocking in the Alabama Hills,
eastern Sierra Nevada Mountains

Boondocking – Camping Outside the Box

"Life is either a daring adventure or nothing at all." –Helen Keller

When my husband first told me about boondocking, I pictured getting "stuck" in some scary, remote location in the "boonies", without cell reception, and some weirdo camping nearby.

So what is this "off the grid" kind of camping?

It's been described as camping outside developed campgrounds, on federal public land (except where restricted), in remote locations for FREE! Sometimes called "dispersed camping" or "pirate camping", we like to find a secluded spot, usually about a mile or two away from developed campgrounds and not too close to other boondockers. New US Forest Service dispersed camping rules have come out and each forest may have different requirements so be sure to check locally. Keep in mind camping closer than 300 ft. of a water source is usually restricted.

Over the years I have grown to LOVE boondocking!

Sometimes you'll even find FREE overnight RV parking places at Wal-Mart, Camping World or truck stops.

Boondocking Etiquette

1. Use Existing Roads & Camping Spots

2. Pack It In, Pack It Out

3. Pay Attention To Stay Limits (typically 14-days within 28-day period)

4. Keep A Respectful Distance From Your Neighbor

5. Be Neighborly About Pets & Noise

6. Be Sociable, Be Private... (common sense prevails)

7. Share The Land

Boondock camping in northwestern Nevada

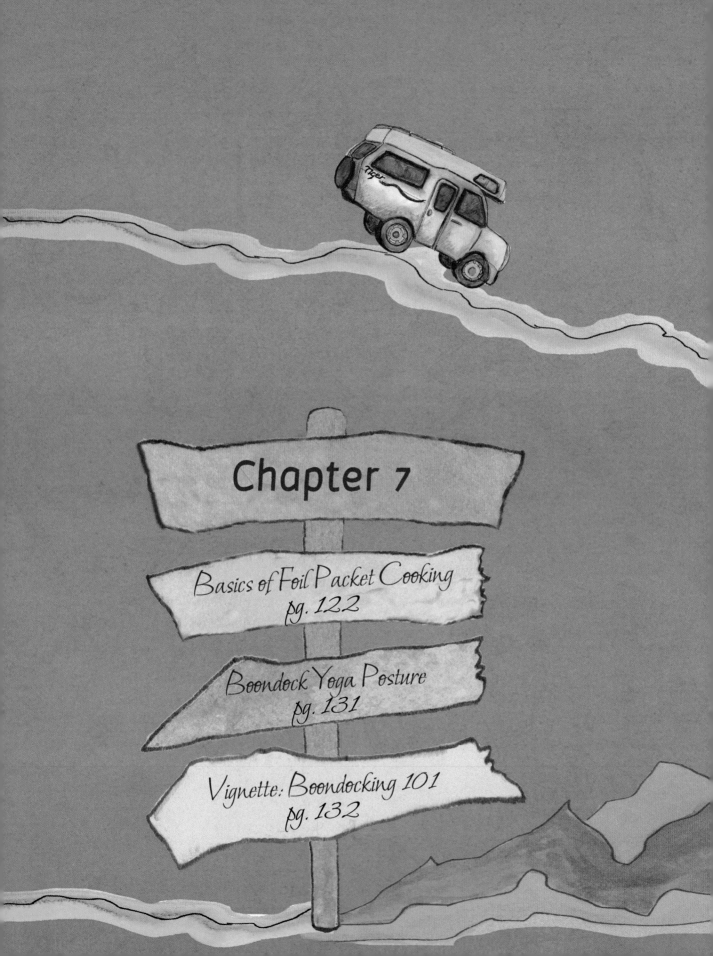

Chapter 7

7
Foil Packet Recipes

Fantastic Foil Packet Meal Basics and Safety Tips

- Use **Heavy Duty Aluminum Foil**—the ultimate secret weapon when cooking on a campfire. If using regular weight use 2 layers of foil.

    - Also pack a box of parchment paper to line all your foil packets to avoid aluminum toxicity.

- CAUTION: We all need to Reduce our Aluminum Exposure

    - Aluminum is a heavy metal like lead and can be toxic in excessive amounts. Excess cooking with aluminum foil can affect bone density. Aluminum can build up inside bones and reduce calcium levels. When aluminum foil is heated it emits parts of the metal that can leech into the food.

- When using foil pack recipes simply wrap food in parchment paper first, and then surround it with the foil packet.

- If you don't want to use any aluminum foil, wrap food in parchment paper and place the packets in a Dutch oven surrounded by hot coals.

- Always use potholders or tongs to move packets. Foil heats quickly!

- Airtight foil packets will steam the contents. Be very careful when opening to prevent burning your hand.

- Cook some foods over direct heat – placing packets directly over heat source. *Rotate packet occasionally.*

- Some foods cook better over indirect heat. Place packets on cool side of grill or heat source.

- "Tent" packets work best for steaming and less browning. Here's how to fold the packet into a tent:

    - Cut one piece of foil long enough to wrap around the food with enough left over to fold the top and side edges in the middle. Leave room at top between food and foil for steaming.

    - I found it works better to make a few smaller packets rather than one large packet. Food cooks faster and more evenly.

- In a pinch you can even use foil to make a baking pan. Double up sheets of foil and mold it over an upside down pan or plate of choice. Crimp edges well for strength.

Roasted Potato and Fennel Packets

Try to cut potatoes all about the same size so they roast evenly. I make these frequently because they're so easy to make and don't forget the sliced fennel! They blend well with potatoes and garlic. Leftovers are great with eggs the next morning. Serves 4

- 1 large red onion

- ¾ lb. potatoes, chopped in wedges (I used red, purple and fingerling potatoes)

- 1 ½ medium fennel bulbs, cored & thinly sliced

- ¼ cup olive oil

- 2-3 large cloves garlic

- 1 Tbsp. Dijon mustard

- 1 tsp. sea salt

- 1 tsp. fresh ground pepper

- Chopped fresh parsley for garnish

1. Mix the onions, potato, and fennel slices in large bowl.

2. Stir in olive oil, garlic, mustard, salt and pepper. Toss well.

3. Divide the vegetables evenly among 4 squares of aluminum foil, lined with parchment paper. Wrap into packets, leaving room for heat to circulate inside.

4. Cook on grill over high heat, 30–35 minutes, or until veggies are tender.

5. Open packets and sprinkle parsley on top before serving.

Sweet and Spicy Sweet Potato Packets

This is one of my favorite side dishes. Don't forget the cinnamon and ground cumin spices to add some intense aroma and flavor!

- 2 sweet potatoes cut in 1 inch cubes
- 1 bell peppers – any color, cut into 1½ inch cubes
- 1 red onion cut in wedges
- 2 Tbsp. melted coconut oil
- ¼ tsp. ground cumin
- ¼ tsp. paprika
- ¼ tsp. cinnamon
- ½ tsp. sea salt
- ¼ tsp. ground pepper

1. In a large bowl or re-sealable plastic bag, toss or shake sweet potatoes, peppers, and onion with oil, and spices.

2. Divide potatoes evenly among 4 squares of aluminum foil and wrap in to packets, leaving room for heat to circulate inside.

3. Cook on grill over high heat, 30–35 minutes, or until veggies are tender.

Nutrition Tip

These orange spuds can help regulate glucose, or blood sugar, while also offering important antioxidants to ward off chronic diseases. Sweet potatoes are ranked lower than white potatoes on the Glycemic Index and they may help people with diabetes better manage their blood sugar levels.

The orange flesh varieties are packed with beta-carotene that converts to Vitamin A to promote eye health. High vitamin C content helps build our immune system. They're also a great source of Fiber to make us feel full longer.

Foil Wrapped Pork Tenderloin

Hoisin sauce, sesame oil and maple syrup bake into a crisp coating for this easy roast pork. Use dark toasted sesame oil for this dish—it gives an Asian flavor.

2-3 servings

- ⅛ cup maple syrup
- ⅛ cup gluten-free Hoisin sauce (see Tip below)
- 1 Tbsp. toasted sesame oil
- 1 pork tenderloin (about 1 lb.)
- 1 medium onion or one large leek thinly sliced
- 3 garlic cloves, peeled and halved
- Salt and pepper

1. Preheat grill or tend campfire till coals have formed. Place grill over coals.

2. Prepare one large piece of parchment paper on top of a piece of aluminum foil the same size.

3. In small bowl, stir together maple syrup, hoisin sauce and sesame oil. Set aside.

4. Rub pork tenderloin with cut side of garlic slice. Spread onions slices and garlic in center of parchment/aluminum paper. Place pork tenderloin on onion and garlic mixture. Sprinkle pork lightly with salt and pepper. Wrap parchment/aluminum paper around pork and onion mixture.

5. Place foil wrapped meat on top of grill or nestle in beside coals of campfire.

6. Roast for about 30-40 minutes – halfway through add hoisin/syrup sauce on top.

7. Before removing from heat check temperature of meat. Roast pork should be at least 145°. Let pork rest 10 minutes. Slice and serve with the onion mixture.

Nutrition Tip:

No Hoisin Sauce?

Make your own! Mix together 2 Tbsp. gluten-free tamari sauce, 2 Tbsp. orange juice, 1 Tbsp. minced ginger root, 1 Tbsp. minced garlic.

Apple Foil Packets

I always double this recipe and if there's any leftover I serve it with savory pancakes for breakfast. Foil roasted apples are a great dessert too with cardamom flavored ice cream.

- 2–3 medium sweet tart apples unpeeled cut into wedges
- 1 Tbsp. olive oil
- ½-1 tsp. Ceylon cinnamon

1. Toss apples, oil and cinnamon together and divide between 2-3 large squares of foil and wrap into packets. Leave room for heat to circulate inside.

2. Cook on grill for 25–35 minutes or until apples are tender.

Foil Pack Dinner Menu:

- Pork tenderloin with onions
- Apple Foil Packets (recipe below)
- Foil packed chopped broccoli and sliced corn off the cob
- 2-3 squares of dark chocolate bar

Mushroom and Lemongrass Packets

These savory herbs and veggies add an incredible Asian flavor to any fish, poultry or beef dish!

- 1-2 cups mushrooms (combination crimini, shitake, and trumpet)
- 2 stalks lemongrass chopped in 1-2 inch chunks (peel outer skin off and after chopping into chunks, smash the lemongrass with hammer or rock, or mallet to release oils)
- 1-2 sliced scallions
- 2-6 whole, peeled cloves of garlic
- Chopped fresh Thai basil or regular basil
- Chopped Thai or jalapeño pepper (optional)
- Drizzle of olive oil
- ½-1 lime or lemon juiced
- Sea salt to taste

1. Toss everything together in a bowl and transfer to foil packet.

2. Roast on grill or near coals for 15 minutes.

3. Try this with Foil Baked Fish, next...

Foil Baked Fish with Mustard Marinade

Hey there fishermen and women—embellish that trout, salmon, cod, snapper or halibut you caught with very tasty recipe! Don't forget the horseradish.

- 1 ½ lbs. favorite fish

Marinade:

- ½ cup Dijon mustard

- ⅓ cup lemon juice

- ½ tsp. dried thyme

- 2 tsp. prepared horseradish

- 2 tsp. lemon zest or peel

- ¼ tsp. ground black pepper & salt

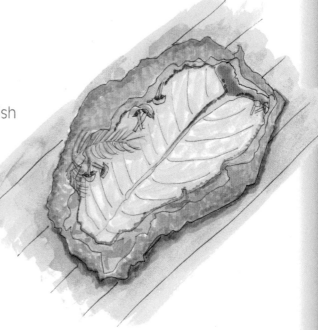

🍄 ⋰ 🍄

1. Marinade fish for 20–60 minutes before cooking. Rinse and dry fish fillets and place them skin side down on a plate or pan.

2. Whisk marinade ingredients together in bowl and pour over fish. Making sure to coat both sides.

3. Ready to cook: Wrap fish in foil packet and place on grill or insert next to coals for 10–15 minutes or until fish is tender and flakes easily with a fork.

Alternative Fish Recipe:

Using your favorite fish try marinating it simply with lemon juice, salt and pepper. Foil bake for 10–15 minute alongside Mushroom and Lemongrass packets (page 129). Serve fish on top of large spoonful baked mushrooms and lemongrass.

Boondock Yoga

I scrambled up that rocky ridge in Death Valley, CA while Bill stayed below and took these photos. Ginger Dog will protect me wherever I go!

131

My First Boondocking Experience

"A world without open country would be universal jail."
-Edward Abbey

We arrived in Death Valley in late October for my first boondocking adventure. The temperatures were still in the upper 80's and low 90's during the day, and not much cooler at night.

We drove right past the National Park campgrounds and turned onto a narrow, gravel/sand road leading into Echo Canyon. Oh my, at that time we were driving our Ford 2-wheel camper van, and I feared we'd get stuck in the sand. Whew, we made it just past the 2 mile requirement from a main highway, and pulled into a wide spot off the road. It didn't feel very private, without trees or large bushes in sight, but I was game for this adventure.

We ended up having an incredible time and stayed for 3 days until our water ran out. Each night after dinner we sat in reclining chairs identifying stars and I saw my first satellite slowly creeping across the desert sky. It was so hot that although we slept inside the van, we kept all doors and windows wide open, basking naked with a warm breeze and coyotes howling. I was hooked on boondocking!

Very few vehicles drove by except when Bill decided to take his outside shower. Of course, as soon as he was all set up and bare-naked, a jeep with 4 folks drove by. Waves of laughter and horn honking filled the air and Bill just acted like nothing unusual was happening. What perfect timing and a perfect location!

Another highlight of this trip was discovering all the rock art created by previous "dockers." I had no idea how much joy comes from drawing and painting with natural desert material. Understandably, new park rules require that these creations be taken apart so others can enjoy the landscape in its natural state. And that's the experience we're all looking for, isn't it?

Chapter 8

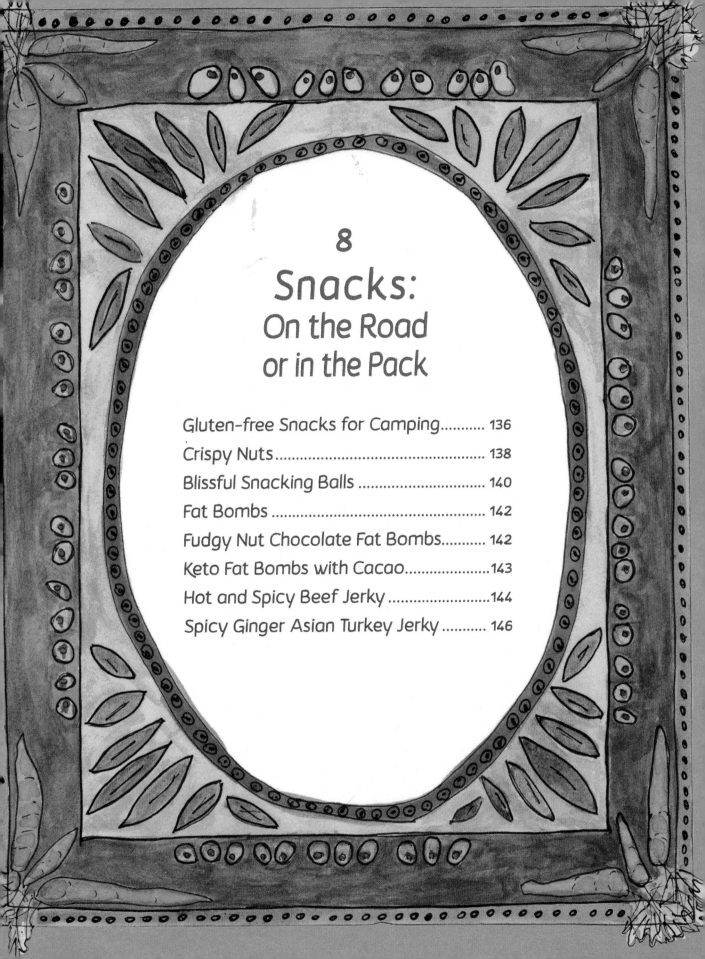

8
Snacks:
On the Road or in the Pack

Gluten-free Snacks for Camping

It only takes a few minutes to prepare a handful of nibbles that you can enjoy when camping. Here are some quick and easy snack ideas to make the most out of your healthy travels.

1. **Homemade GORP** (*acronym that stands for "good old raisins and peanuts"*) also known as trail mix. A great snack for your pack while hiking or away from camp kitchen. My favorite combinations:

   a. Dried pears, figs, raisins, cherries or apples, crispy nuts (recipe page 138), goji berries, sunflower seeds, pumpkin seeds, cacao nibs, candied ginger, dark chocolate chips, or organic M&Ms.

2. Take a **gluten-free tortilla and spread on a dollop of hummus,** avocado slices, grated carrots, fresh arugula and a dollop of hot sauce or avocado cream. Wrap it like a burrito and wrap in parchment paper for an easy snack or meal option.

3. Pack a sleeve of **whole grain rice cakes** like those from Lundberg with a few individual nut butter packets such as **Justin's Nut Butter**. When you're in the mood—simply take out a rice cake and spread the almond butter on top. Add a few thin slices of apple and enjoy!

4. If you find yourself pressed for time, pack **two ripe avocados** in a brown paper bag with sea salt and pepper. Avocados are an easy snack that you can eat with sea salt, pepper and a spoon. If you're not a fan of eating an avocado by itself, pair it with whole grain gluten-free crackers or whole grain rice cakes for a satisfying snack.

5. You can also *hard boil a few eggs* before you travel and bring them with you for a quick protein-packed snack with sea salt and pepper; their combination of healthy fat and protein will hold you over and keep you satisfied.

6. **Fresh organic seasonal fruit** is another convenient option.

7. If you have a sweet tooth, pack a few pitted **Medjool dates** and stuff them with almond butter for a tasty treat anytime of the day or night.

8. You can also chop up your **favorite organic veggies**, such as zucchini, carrots, snow peas and bell peppers and toss them into a sealed bag or container of Curried Hummus (page 50), Green Goddess Dip (page 47), or Chipotle Guacamole (page 51), and you're all set for a mini snack.

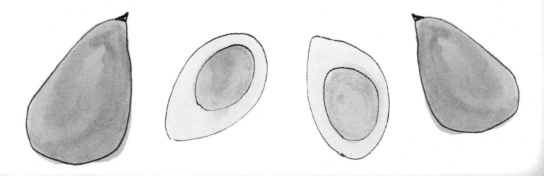

Snack Recipes

Crispy Nuts

Recipe from Nourishing Traditions cookbook by Sally Fallon

The best way to eat nuts and seeds and gain the nutritious benefits is to eat them soaked and dehydrated. Why soak them? Basically it makes them a lot easier to digest but here's a more scientific reason:

Soaking neutralizes the enzyme inhibitors, which make them difficult to digest. It neutralizes the phytates (present in the bran of all grains and seeds), which inhibit the absorption of minerals such as magnesium, calcium, iron, zinc and copper. The germination process increases many nutrients in the nuts and seeds, such as vitamin C, the B vitamins and carotenes. It also produces enzymes.

- 4 cups raw nuts, almonds, walnuts, pecans, cashews, pumpkin seeds, Macadamia nuts

- 1 Tbsp. sea salt

🍄 ⁛ 🍄

1. Mix nuts with salt and enough filtered water to cover. Leave in a warm place for at least 7 hours, or all day/overnight. Cashews are the only exception because they become slimy or develop a disagreeable smell if allowed to soak too long. Soak them in salted water for 6 hours, no longer. Drain in colander. Spread soaked nuts on cookie sheets and place in warm oven (150°-170°) for 12-14 hours, or use a dehydrator set at 145° for 14-18 hours.

2. Again cashews are an exception; they can be baked at 200-250° for 10–12 hours. Crispy nuts can be stored in airtight jars in the cupboard, but walnuts need to be stored in the refrigerator, because they are more susceptible to rancidity.

Son Logan and fiancé Jenna enjoying a snack spread

Blissful Snacking Balls

Makes 30-40 balls

What makes these little treats blissful? The unusual ingredient called Ashwaghanda or Indian Ginseng is considered an adaptogenic herb. It helps us adapt to stress by regulating our hormones. It's also gives us energy and keeps our mind sharp. Sounds like BLISS to me!

- 1 cup almond butter
- ¼ cup raw honey
- 1 Tbsp. vanilla extract
- 1 Tbsp. cacao or unsweetened cocoa powder
- 3 Tbsp. ashwaganda powder
- 1 Tbsp. cinnamon powder
- 1 Tbsp. ginger powder
- 1 Tbsp. cardamom powder
- 1 tsp. garam masala

OPTIONAL:

- ¼ cup raw pumpkin seeds
- ¼ cup dried cranberries
- shredded coconut
- more cacao or hemp seeds for dusting

1. Mix all spices and cacao (or cocoa) powder together in a small bowl. Set aside.

2. In a larger bowl, combine almond butter, vanilla extract, and honey until creamy smooth. Add the spice mixture and mix until well combined.

3. Add optional pumpkin seeds and dried cranberries here if desired. Then roll into desired sized balls. I like to make them pretty small as each little bliss ball is pretty potent.

4. Roll in shredded coconut or hemp seeds, or dust with more cacao (or cocoa).

Store in refrigerator and if feeling stressed OR when you just want a moment of bliss, pop one in your mouth and ENJOY!

Fat Bombs – a satiating snack

As a nutrition consultant I try all sorts of diets to familiarize myself with the latest diet craze. I tried the ketogenic diet—a high fat, moderate protein and VERY low carbohydrate diet (carbohydrates include all fruits, vegetables, grains, legumes and alcohol). It's a great diet to try for 4-6 weeks to lose weight, balance blood sugar, improve mood, memory and cognition, and even help relieve chronic pain. In fact it has been used since the 1920's to treat epilepsy and other seizure disorders.

I lasted for only 2 weeks. I found that it helped stabilize blood sugar swings throughout my day, but this diet is high in fat and VERY low in carbohydrates, and I love too many carbs that are forbidden like sweet potatoes, carrots, and beets.

But I did discover a healthy new snack called Fat Bombs! These little nuggets are a great mid morning or mid afternoon snack to balance blood sugar and feel satiated until the next meal. Make them at home and store in refrigerator or cooler so they don't melt. There are many recipes for Fat Bombs. Here are two of my favorites.

Fudgy Nut Chocolate Fat Bombs

- 2 oz. (58gr) Cocoa Butter (*sometimes called cacao butter*)
- 2 Tbsp. unsweetened cocoa or cacao powder
- 2 Tbsp. erythritol (*a natural sugar alcohol*)
- 4 oz. (112gr) chopped macadamias or almonds
- ¼ cup coconut oil
- ¼ cup chia seeds (optional)
- **(Optional for texture)** Handful of cacao nibs, a few drops of food grade peppermint oil, chopped fresh ginger root.

1. Melt cocoa butter in a double boiler (or place a smaller saucepan inside of a larger one filled with 2-3 inches of water)
2. Add cocoa powder to the saucepan and whisk till smooth.
3. Add the erythritol and mix well until all ingredients are well blended and melted.
4. Add macadamias or almonds, chopped ginger or peppermint drops and stir.

5.   Sprinkle with cacao nibs if desired

6.   Add coconut oil and optional chia seeds, mix well until melted

7.   Line a 8"x8" square pan with parchment paper or paper cups, and pour mixture in. Chill in refrigerator and when hard, cut into squares and store in fridge.

Keto Fat Bombs With Cacao

- •   1 cup coconut oil
- •   1 cup almond butter
- •   ¼ cup coconut flour
- •   ½ cup cacao powder
- •   (*Optional added texture*) goji berries, coconut flakes, nuts, or cacao nibs)

🍄 ⁙ 🍄

Heat the coconut oil and almond butter in saucepan over medium heat, and stir until mixed evenly. Stir in the coconut flour and cacao powder, and pour into 8"x8" square pan lined with parchment paper. Add optional texture above, and chill in refrigerator until set enough to cut into squares.

Hot and Spicy Beef Jerky

Every time I prepare these potent snacks before a trip we both comment how satiating they are when hiking or experiencing low blood sugar. In other words, whenever we're really "Hangry"(hungry + possibly angry). Here are two of my favorite recipes.

- 3 lb. lean beef (*I used tri-tip & asked butcher to slice it ¼ in. thick*)
- 1 cup apple cider (or unsweetened apple juice)
- ½ cup balsamic vinegar
- 2 Tbsp. fish sauce (optional)
- ¼ cup Dijon mustard
- ¼ cup unpasteurized honey
- 2 Tbsp. ground black pepper
- 2 Tbsp. smoked paprika
- 3 Tbsp. garlic powder
- 1 Tbsp. onion powder
- 1 Tbsp. Himalayan salt
- 3 Tbsp. sesame oil
- 2 Tbsp. crushed chili pepper
- ¼ tsp. ground clove

🍄 ⫶ 🍄

1. Remove all traces of visible fat from your piece (or pieces) of meat. Place the meat in the freezer for about 60 to 90 minutes, which will make it easier to slice thinly. Don't wait until the meat is frozen solid, but it should be really firm to pierce it with the point of a sharp knife.

2. Slice the meat in long thin strips against the grain. Jerky sliced against the grain tends to be easier to chew and breaks more easily into pieces.

3. Place your meat in a re-sealable plastic bag, or non-reactive container with fitting lid, and set aside.

4. In a large measuring cup or mixing bowl, add all the ingredients for the marinade and mix until very well combined. Pour over the sliced meat and mix everything around until all the strips are completely covered.

5. Place your meat in the refrigerator and let it marinate overnight.

6. The next day using a food dehydrator put jerky on dehydrator trays and dry for 3-5 hours (check on these they dry fast) at 145 degrees.

7. Marinated strips could also be dried in regular oven at lowest temperature for less time. Check them at 3 hours.

Hiking with Fah Sky in the Alabama Hills

Spicy Ginger Asian Turkey Jerky

Honey, ginger and garlic combine for a savory sweet, Asian inspired turkey jerky.

- 3 lb. turkey breasts or turkey tenderloins
- 1 Tbsp. honey
- 4–5 cloves of garlic, chopped
- 1½ inch chunk of fresh ginger, scrubbed & chopped
- 1 Tbsp. sea salt
- 2 Tbsp. gluten free tamari
- 1-2 Tbsp. balsamic vinegar (coconut balsamic is sensational)
- ½ -1 tsp. chili flakes
- Ground black pepper to taste

1. Salt and pepper the strips of meat in a bowl.

2. Mix honey, garlic, ginger, tamari, vinegar and chili flakes.

3. Add marinade to meat and smoosh it with your hands to cover every piece.

4. Put the meat mixture in a ziplock plastic bag and allow to marinate over night.

5. Put the strips of meat on a dehydrator tray and dehydrate at 155 degrees until dry but still bendy. About 4-5 hours.

6. Marinated strips could also be dried in regular oven at lowest temperature for less time. Check them at 3 hours.

Snack Pack Yoga

After SNACKING on the beach, I tried to find balance on a cantilevered log.

WHOA . . . . . Don't fall!

Boondock Meltdown

*"All journeys have secret destinations
of which the traveler is unaware."*
–Martin Buber

Wind sucks! Don't get me wrong I love weather. And I love change. But when weather changes to constant wind, and we're spending most of our day outdoors, wind can be VERY annoying.

In fact on one trip it was so windy for two days, I had a backcountry meltdown.

We had spent a second day hiking and struggling with strong currents. On our way out of a dry river canyon, using walking sticks and plenty of lip balm, we marched with heads down, hat brims flipping up every time we tried to look up, and tiny particles of sand pelting our face for 2.5 miles. Was this supposed to be fun?

We finally made it back to the camper, ready to relax and find a quiet, protected place to recover and camp for the night. That turned out to be a fantasy.

It was so windy; every place we tried to set up camp was blustering. At one secluded spot, the camper started rocking back and forth and I felt nauseous and hangry (hungry + angry).

I wanted a plan, an agenda, an outline of what was going to happen next! This boondocker was turning into a "looney docker" and was not a "happy camper." I sank into a grimacing silence.

Sweetheart Bill read my mind (It probably wasn't hard at that point!) and quickly came up with an idea.

Luckily, we were not far from the sweet little town of Boulder, Utah, along the Escalante Grand Staircase. We pulled into the Boulder Mountain Lodge just in time to score the last room in the house. By then, I would have been content in a cheap, seedy motel.

But, what a surprise to find ourselves in an upscale resort, including a whole foods, sustainable restaurant called Hell's Backbone Grill. It felt heavenly to soak in the hot tub, savor organic vegetables and pasture-raised poultry, and sleep in a king-sized bed! Filled with gratitude, we embraced our freedom to choose a perfect way to replenish! I LOVE change! (Wink, wink)

photo by David Heaton

Chapter 9

9
Desserts

Campfire Desserts

The easiest and perhaps the healthiest dessert for us is a couple of squares of an organic dark chocolate bar with at least 70% cacao.

Dark Chocolate Nutrition Tip

Not all chocolate is created equal. The health benefits of processed, highly sweetened chocolate are few, but the benefits of dark chocolate with over 70% cacao are numerous and quite impressive. Dark chocolate's cocoa has been shown to have a very high content of antioxidants - compounds that neutralize free radicals and protect the body from their damage. So the higher the cacao/cocoa percentage of your next dark chocolate bar, the more awesome antioxidants you'll consume. The flavonoids in chocolate not only help prevent cancer but they also reduce blood pressure, improve blood flow and increase cognitive function.

Dutch Oven Apple Crisp

This was the first thing I made in my Dutch oven and it turned out heavenly. For this dessert we cooked it right in the campfire ring with pre-heated briquettes.

Apple Mixture:

- 5 cups chopped apples (or a combination apple/pear, nectarine/blueberry, or strawberry/rhubarb)
- 1 tsp. Ceylon cinnamon
- ½ tsp. ground cardamom
- Coconut oil spray

Topping:

- ½ cup gluten-free rolled oats, almond meal or gluten free granola
- ½ cup all purpose gluten-free flour (see gluten-free flour blend below)
- ¼ – ½ cup chopped almonds

- ¼ cup maple syrup

- ¼ cup pastured butter (I like Kerrygold unsalted)

- Pinch of salt

- ¼ cup shredded raw coconut.

- (*Optional*) 1-2 Tbsp. lemon zest

🍄 ⁝⁝ 🍄

1. Spray bottom and sides of Dutch oven with coconut spray.

2. Spread apple mixture in bottom of 12 inch Dutch oven.

3. Combine topping ingredients and spread over apples. Bake at 350° for 25–30 minutes, using 8 coals under and 16 on lid.

4. Continue cooking until apples are cooked and topping is brown.

5. Serve warm or cold with vanilla coconut bliss or whipped cream.

Gluten–free flour Blend: I like to use ⅓ part cassava flour, ⅓ part tapioca or arrowroot flour and ⅓ part almond meal or flour)

Banana Boat Packets

Oh I wish my father was still living to enjoy this delicious dessert. "Johnny" loved banana split hot fudge sundaes, but in those days we didn't understand the damaging affects of sugar. There are a lot of recipes for Campfire Banana Boats but most contain chocolate chips and marshmallows. I wanted to create a healthy version of this camping classic. Personally I think these are pretty sweet but others may want to add more chocolate chips or squares of dark chocolate.

Ingredients for one serving:

- 1 banana
- 2 tsp. dark chocolate chips or break up 2 squares of dark chocolate
- 1 Tbsp. shredded unsweetened coconut (or try toasted coconut flakes)
- 1 Tbsp. chopped toasted hazelnuts or almonds
- Dash of ground cinnamon, to taste
- Small pinch of sea salt

Garnish options:

- Served with coconut milk ice cream + topped with goji berries
- Dried mulberries + almond butter
- Dash of cinnamon and cayenne + almond butter

154

1. Heat your grill or enjoy the experience of making these over an open fire (using a grill rack over the fire pit)

2. Using a sharp knife cut the banana in half, keeping the peel, and gently opening from the slit. Place the split banana on a large piece of foil, and top with dark chocolate chips, coconut, hazelnuts, cinnamon and sea salt in the opening of the banana, where it's been cut.

3. Next wrap the foil around the banana making sure that all the contents are tightly wrapped around and won't pour out of the foil over the flame.

4. Next place the foil wrapped banana on the open flame or grill and cook for 5-8 minutes or until the banana is soft and chocolate is melted (check by opening the foil and stabbing with a fork).

5. Serve hot with a dollop of coconut ice cream or crème fraîche and enjoy!

Katie's Cookies

Chocolate, Coconut, Cranberry & Gluten free!

Before I opened my yoga studio in 1995, I was debating whether to open Katie's Cookie Cart instead. I guess you know the answer to that one. I ran Wild Mountain Yoga Center for 12 years before going back to school to become a certified nutrition consultant. From my studies at nutrition school, I made the decision to just STOP baking!

I use to bake cookies or another "healthy" dessert every week using whole-wheat flour and honey. Bill and our boys were packing lunches each day so there were never any leftovers. Over time we all developed quite a sweet tooth. Treats made with honey and whole-wheat flour have the same effect on our body as white flour and white sugar. They spike our blood sugar and I understand now that SUGAR causes inflammation in our body and inflammation is at the root of most diseases.

Literally I just stopped baking . . . . until I felt we had our sugar cravings under control which took about 5 years. OH MY! Now I bake occasionally, but everything is gluten–free and very low in sugar. So they aren't as addicting as goodies made with white sugar and white flour because quite frankly they don't have the same addictive quality. You can actually eat just one and feel satiated. But. . . these cookies are a real treat for me now!

Ingredients:

- 1 cup Otto's Naturals Casava flour (or ½ gluten-free flour of choice and ½ gluten-free rolled oats). **Other gluten-free flours:** arrowroot, tapioca, coconut or almond flour

- ½ cup dried coconut flakes

- 1 tsp. baking soda

- ¼ tsp. sea salt

- 6 Tbsp. unsalted pastured butter or coconut oil (room temperature)

- 5 Tbsp. honey or maple syrup

- 2 large eggs

- ½ cup dark chocolate chips

- ⅓ cup dried cranberries

- ⅓ cup dried raisins

- ⅓ cup nuts (*I like the texture of whole almonds or walnuts*)

- 2 tsp. grated or zested orange rind

1. Preheat oven to 325°F. Line 2 large baking sheets with parchment paper.

2. In a medium bowl whisk together the flour, dried coconut flakes, baking soda and salt.

3. In a large mixing bowl beat together the softened butter (or coconut oil) and honey with electric mixer until smooth. Add eggs and beat until combined.

4. Add flour mixture to egg and butter mixture and beat to form dough. Stir in chocolate chips, dried cranberries, raisins, nuts and orange rind.

5. Drop tablespoons of dough on to baking sheets about 2 inches apart. Bake for about 12-15 minutes till golden brown and centers are set. Cool completely on baking sheet and store in airtight container.

Chocolate Coconut Fondue

Forget the marshmallows! Try this chocolate fondue with fresh fruit dippers.

- 1 can full fat coconut milk
- 2 tsp. pure vanilla extract
- 1 tsp. ground Ceylon cinnamon
- ¼ tsp. cayenne powder (optional)
- Pinch of salt
- 5-6 oz. dark chocolate (70%) cacao, finely chopped
- Dippers of choice (fresh strawberries, banana hunks, wedges of fresh peach, plum, pear, figs, mango, apricots or cantaloupe)

🍄 ⋮ 🍄

Optional to make at home or at camp: Prepare coconut cream: Place coconut milk can in refrigerator and chill overnight. Without shaking the can, scoop out the thick coconut cream on top and place it in a small jar along with vanilla, cinnamon, cayenne (if using) and salt. Mash mixture together, seal jar and transport in cooler.

At camp: In a small saucepan, melt coconut cream mixture over medium fire. Stir in chopped chocolate. Remove from heat and let sit, covered for 2 minutes. Stir until mixture is uniformly dark. Place dippers on a stick or skewer and dip in warm chocolate.

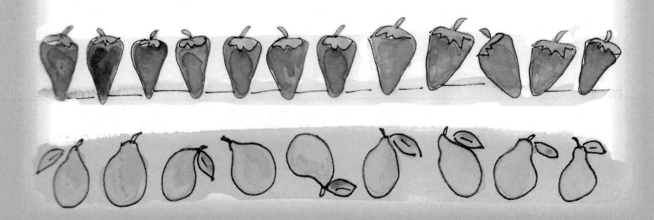

Yoga Sweetness

Andrew Rogers' land art sculpture "The Ratio" *sits on a hill, off Interstate 70, in Green River, Utah. "The Ratio" is based on the Fibonacci sequence, a mathematical concept of universal significance similar to the Golden Ratio of science and mathematics. This sequence is found in numerous patterns in nature.*

Practicing yoga on a stack of sugar cubes

Finding Common Ground in the Backcountry

*"Traveling has humbled me and has broadened
my perspective in so many ways".*
—Anonymous

For the past 9 years, I've learned a lot about 4-wheelin' remote backcountry roads.

At times I'm white knuckling the handgrips as our camper tilts right, then left while bumping over rocks and giant potholes.

Sometimes I wonder how much longer I can endure both the thrill and fear of surviving in the wilderness. It's no surprise that most of the folks we meet while boondocking are either single adventurous men of all ages or young fit couples.
It's hard as a woman in my 60's to wonder where I fit in.

One night at a very remote campground in Capital Reef National Park in Utah, we camped near 2 single, 4-wheeling guys who were traveling separately. While Bill exchanged stories with the men about their travels and vehicles, I headed to our kitchen to prepare a Dutch-oven apple crisp. **(See recipe page 152.)** Earlier that day we had picked a bagful of apples in the town of Fruita, Utah—a Mormon settlement known for their orchards and preserved under the National Park Service.

As our dessert baked, I invited the two traveling strangers to join our camp-fire after dinner for my home-baked treat. One guy was 20 something from Switzerland on a solo tour of the US in his Land Rover "tricked out" Expedition vehicle. He was writing and posting a travel blog of his journey and had great tales to share. The other guy, about our age, was from Arizona; traveling in an older re-modeled 4-wheel drive truck and cab. His laid back personality explained why he was taking his time exploring southern Utah.

Although we all came from different backgrounds, we shared a common respect for the solitude and vast expansive wilderness of America's western states. And whether traveling solo, with a partner or friends it's a welcome delight to share a homemade dessert around a fire. DING! I was beginning to discover where I fit in to this world of backcountry explorers. My creative feminine spirit came alive knowing I brought traveling souls together with home baked goodness, a campfire and rich conversation.

We all felt the common ground found in our shared love for Mother Nature, survival, nourishment and community. Perhaps our commonalities actually do outweigh our differences and there is hope for humanity.

Dutch Oven Apple Crisp baking in campfire ring.

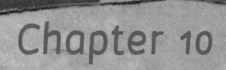

Chapter 10

10
Beverages

Healthy Beverage Ideas

Hydration. When traveling it can be difficult to drink enough water. We're always checking the level on our camper's 30-gallon water tank and practice preservation all the time.

We treat Water like GOLD when boondocking.

Check out **Dishwashing Tips in a Tiny Camp Kitchen**, page 170.

Long ago we traded addictive sugary sodas, diet sodas and fruit juices for truly refreshing plain or mineral water with lime, fruit-infused waters or organic black, white, hibiscus teas or my new favorite—SPORTea (see page 169). Mineral water can be helpful for balancing electrolytes, while teas are loaded with anti-oxidants and contain other beneficial and medicinal qualities.

Commercially sweetened beverages are a multi million-dollar industry in the US. The industry adds sugar, food dyes, processed junk or even worse—artificial sweeteners to flavor water! Stay away from these—they ignite our sweet tooth and wipe out healthy micro biome (friendly bacteria in our digestive tract).

If you want to add some delicious taste and health benefits to water, try these healthy beverage recipes instead! These recipes use micronutrient-rich herbs, fruits, and vegetables for thirst-quenching flavor with added benefits and without the damaging effects of sugar. These are surprisingly tasty, making it easier to drink more water to stay hydrated.
Variety is the spice of life, after all!

1. **Kombucha Tea cocktail** – Kombucha is a fermented beverage that encourages the growth of friendly bacteria. It needs to be stored cold so I only bring a few bottles. Most groceries stores carry kombucha tea in many flavors.

   a. Add ¼ cup of kombucha tea to ¼ cup mineral water or herb ice tea with a wedge of lime, sprig of rosemary and float some berries on top – voila!

   b. *Happy Hour Variation:* add a shot of vodka, tequila or gin! Serve in a wine glass.

2. **Artisanal Vinegar cocktail**

   a. Add 1 tsp. artisanal vinegar (*found at specialty cooking stores – blueberry, pineapple, balsamic vinaigrette*) to 1-cup plain water or mineral water.

   b. Serve in wine glass.

3. Mineral water with a splash of pomegranate juice or tart cherry juice.

4. **Fruit-Infused Water** – All recipes are for ½ gallon mason jar of filtered water. Steep them in shade, on kitchen counter or refrigerator for at least 4 hours or over night. There are endless other combinations of fruit. Try whatever you have on hand!

   a. **Cucumber Mint:** Add one thinly sliced cucumber to a ½ gallon glass jar or water, add 8 muddled fresh mint leaves.

   b. **Citrus Blueberry:** Thinly slice two oranges including rinds and add to ½ gallon jar of water with 1-cup blueberries.

c. **Pineapple Mint:** Peel and thinly slice about ¼ of a pineapple. Add 10-12 leaves of muddled fresh mint.

d. **Watermelon Basil:** Add about 2 cups of finely chopped fresh watermelon (without rind). Add 15 leaves of muddled basil.

e. **Strawberry Lemon:** Add 15 fresh strawberries, with one sliced lemon with rind on.

f. **Cherry Lime:** Add two cups of fresh cherries, cut in half, and one fresh lime, sliced into thin slices.

5. **Hibiscus Cooler:**

a. Make your own at camp. Add 4-6 hibiscus tea bags (they come in many flavors) to a half-gallon jar of water. Leave in sun all day while playing outside.

b. Hibiscus tea tastes wonderful and has a flavor sort of like cranberry. But there are countless ways to jazz this tea up:

    i. **A Little Sweet:** add 1 drop of liquid stevia per cup

    ii. **Citrus Zest:** Lemon, lime, orange or grapefruit slices.

    iii. **Cherry Pucker:** 1 tablespoon of tart cherry juice per cup. Tart cherries are extremely anti-inflammatory.

Nutrition Tip

Hibiscus tea contains more antioxidants than green tea and supports healthy aging. It may help lower blood pressure, aid weight loss, improve heart and liver health and even help fight cancer and bacteria.

Beverage Recipes

Healthy Campfire Hot Cocoa

Commercial hot cocoa is usually loaded with sugar (about 12 grams per cup) and other unpronounceable ingredients that I doubt are very natural. So why not make your own healthy version and enjoy all the benefits too? *1 serving*.

- 1 heaping Tbsp. unsweetened cocoa or cacao powder.

- 1–1 ½ cups water, coconut, or almond milk

- 1 stick cinnamon (optional)

- 1–2 tsp. xylitol or 2-3 drops liquid stevia, or 1 Tbsp. maple syrup or honey

1. Heat water or coconut/almond milk and simmer on low with cinnamon stick. (No need to simmer if not using spice).

2. Whisk cocoa powder in mug with just 1 Tbs. of hot liquid till forms a paste.

3. Add hot water/milk to cocoa paste and add to cocoa mixture.

4. Add a few drops of stevia or1 Tbsp. maple syrup or honey.

5. Sprinkle with more cinnamon, nutmeg or cardamom if desired.

6. You could also add ½ to 1 scoop of protein powder for a late afternoon snack.

Nutrition Tip

Hot Cocoa has a lot more to offer than just a guilty pleasure! Unsweetened Cocoa is rich in minerals like iron, magnesium, calcium, selenium, potassium and zinc. It offers anti-inflammatory and antioxidant qualities as well as relief from high blood pressure, cholesterol, obesity, constipation, blood sugar imbalance and also possesses mood enhancing properties. Pour me another cup please!

Iced Green Matcha (Latte)

A surprising afternoon pick-me- up! And I'm not kidding!

- 1 tsp. ceremonial grade organic matcha
- 1 cup of almond milk or other nut milk (I use half coconut milk and half water)
- 2 tsp. brain octane oil (MCT oil) optional
- 1 tsp. honey, maple syrup or 2-3 drops stevia

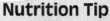

1. Blend in your shaker cup and enjoy served on ice.

2. This can also be made hot. Just heat 12 oz. of a combination of water and nut milk and add other ingredients. When this is heated you can swap MCT oil with regular coconut oil.

Nutrition Tip

Matcha is a great coffee alternative with tons of health benefits. Chock full of antioxidants, some studies show it may help fight inflammation in the body.

It also contains a unique amino acid called L-theanine, which can help with relaxation and anxiety, by producing a "feel-good" state of mind. Although matcha contains more caffeine than green tea, it does not give you the jittery feeling that can occur when you drink coffee. Enjoy!

What's MCT oil?

MCT stands for Medium-Chain Triglycerides.

This high-octane form of coconut oil is excellent for boosting energy and supporting your metabolism and brain health. It's known as a "good" fat that needs less energy and enzymes to be digested so it's a readily accessible energy source. Try adding a teaspoon or two to your smoothies or hot coffee for long lasting fuel and feeling satiated.

SPORTea®: Quick and Easy Ice Tea

*My latest tea discovery is **SPORTea®**: a blend of green and black teas (less than 2% caffeine), Siberian Eleuthero root, ginger, Mate and vitamin C. It comes packaged in large tea bags that make a perfect quart of tea to replenish electrolytes and trace minerals.*

Simply add one tea bag to a quart jar of water and set in the sun for 4 hours or overnight on your kitchen counter.

Add some ice and enjoy this invigorating and replenishing drink!

Nutrition Tip

WATER, WATER, WATER

Even healthy eaters often underestimate the importance of water intake and wind up suffering from chronic, low-grade dehydration. The golden rule of hydration is to drink about half your body weight in ounces of non-alcoholic or non-caffeinated liquid.

Make sure water is filtered or spring water. Both fluoride and chloride (added to city water or potable campground water) are chemicals not benficial for our brain.

Water is essential for lubricating your joints, flushing out waste products, and making hormones and neurotransmitters (chemical messengers for the brain).

If we don't stay hydrated, research has discovered that performance in tasks requiring attention, memory, and physical performance are diminished when you are even 2% dehydrated.

Make it a priority to drink enough water each day!!!

Dishwashing Tips in a Tiny Camp Kitchen

WATER CONSERVATION is most IMPORTANT! Our camper has a 30-gallon water tank and built-in hot water heater. On longer trips we carry extra water, but we always try to conserve water.

Always use **BIO-DEGRADABLE SOAP!** We like Camp suds.

Try not to use every dish or pot in the house. I'm guilty of this and make a conscious effort to wipe out bowls and knives and reuse them while cooking.

NEVER STACK DIRTY DISHES! Wipe out any extra leftover food or sauce on plates with paper towels. Stacking dirty dishes makes them greasy and dirty on both sides.

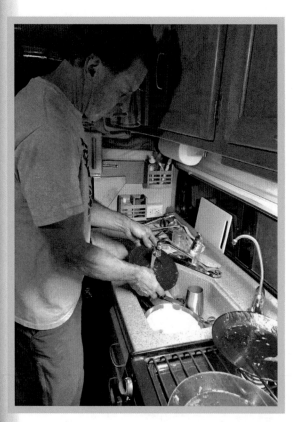

Car camping? To wash dishes use two containers filled about half way – one for soapy water and one for rinse water. While eating dinner, heat a kettle of water for clean up. Wash dishes in soapy water and rinse in rinse water.

In a camper: use biggest pot or bowl and fill with hot soapy water. Wash each dish and place to one side of sink. When all dishes are washed- rinse dishes with faucet or fill one large cup with rinse water and rinse soapy dishes individually before stacking.

My dad taught me to always *wash silverware and glassware first*. They're the first things that touch your lips and should be washed with the cleanest dishwater.

Arrange clean, wet dishes upside down on towel, table or counter. *Air-dry or wipe dishes with dry towel.*

Quench Your Thirst with this Nourishing Yoga Posture

At a campground near Westport, CA (north of Fort Bragg) using a towel as my mat and a scarf as a strap, I stretched my hamstrings; pointing my leg up toward the sky. That's Highway 1 to my left.

Words from Wild Ranger Bill

It's fitting that I'm camping alone in the high Sierras under electric gold-colored aspens making their way toward winter as I write about my life with Katie! So many times we have shared campsites like this during the many stages of our lives.

Almost 44 years ago I was living alone in a cabin nestled under overhanging redwoods in a wildlife sanctuary on the side of Mount Tamalpias. Into my life came a bubble of love and energy unlike anyone I'd yet met. To our relationship we each brought very different personalities and skills but we just seemed to fit and complement each other. It was so easy to just "be" together.

Soon we bought raw land, started businesses, got married, built a home and garden, had two wonderful boys/men and always made time to camp. Throughout all of this time, Katie's love of yoga and health through eating nourishing foods has inspired our family and our whole community.

She is always helping others, using her knowledge to teach and mentor our family, her students and now all of you that pick up this book.

Camping has always been my way to sink back into nature and myself, leaving our civilized "culture" behind. This started with backpacking trips deep into the mountains and then morphed into family car/van /RV trips. As the logistics of backpacking became too difficult with our young family, we made sure our vehicle trips took us to remote and off-the-grid locations. To be in nature and away from the human altered environment has always been my focus.

Blending this alone time with Katie and her influences has deepened my camping experiences both emotionally and most definitely gastronomically. But I must admit, when I camp alone, I eat very simply. I buy prepared salads, grass-fed animal protein and snacks from the health food store. If weather permits I barbecue meat, but otherwise I don't make a big deal out of eating, which makes me REALLY appreciate the meals Katie prepares on our trips together.

Throughout all our years together we continue to do the dance of combining our different skills and personalities into a healthy, well-fed and flexible relationship. Nowhere is that more evident than on camping trips, both alone and together, surrounded by nature, eating delightful and nourishing foods and just "BEING" ourselves.

Bill camping on Klamath River, CA.

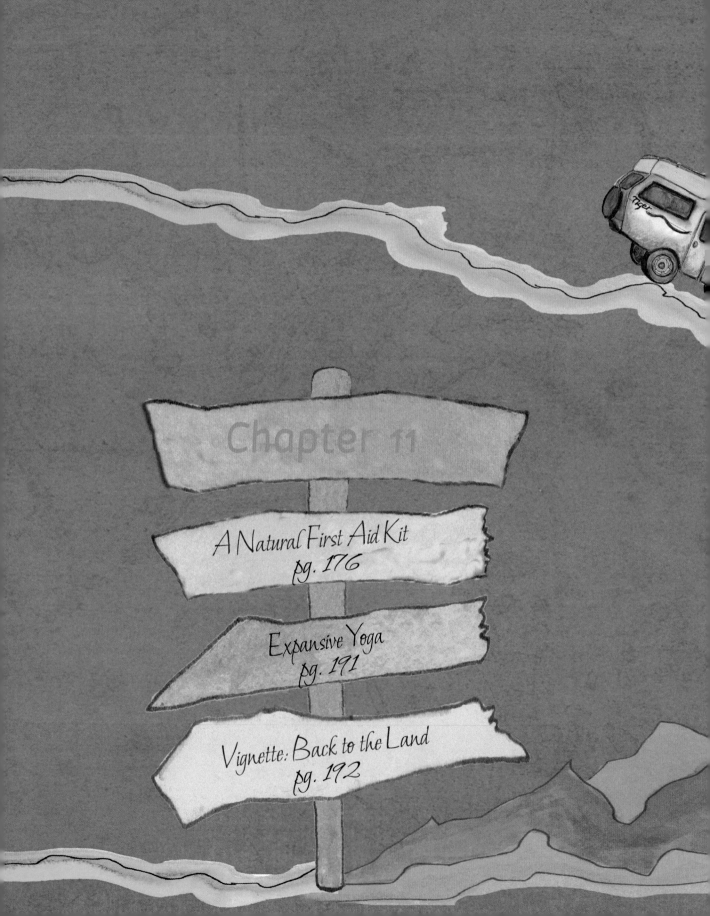

Chapter 11

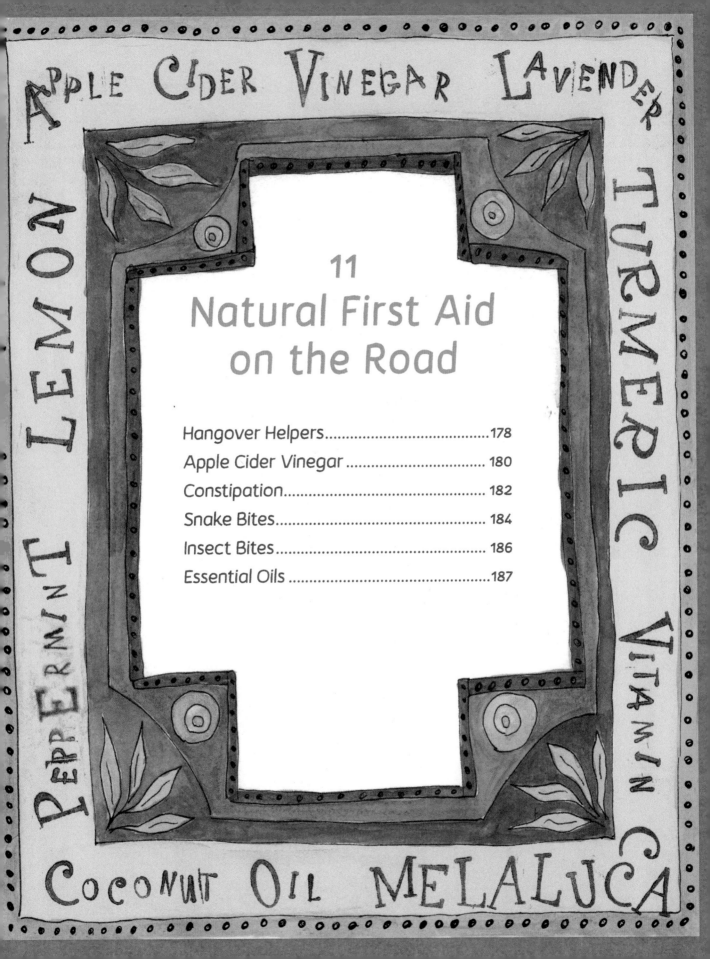

11
Natural First Aid on the Road

Natural First Aid on the Road

Getting injured or feeling sick is not fun, and especially not convenient when on the road. It's well worth being prepared just in case. I always bring a small first aid kit with bandages and anti bacterial cream but I also stock many other natural ingredients, essential oils and products to help heal my body from blisters, stings, bites, scrapes, sprains, splinters, ticks, muscle aches and headaches.

My Natural First Aid Kit includes:
(*see descriptions of each throughout this chapter*)

- Variety of bandages, tweezers and small scissors
- **APPLE CIDER VINEGAR** - Soothe a Sunburn, heal poison ivy, halt a cold or sore throat, loosen constipation
- **TIGER BALM** for headaches and achy muscles.
- **BUFFERED VITAMIN C** – boost immune function, help constipation
- **MAGNESIUM CITRAMATE** – Soothes achy muscles, leg cramps, and reduce constipation. Take at least 400mg before bed.
- **OIL OF OREGANO** – anti-viral and antibacterial. I bring a dietary supplement with 60 mg of oregano oil. If I feel a cold or flu coming on I start with 1 capsule. I may take another capsule before bed. Or try a few drops of an essential oil called Protective Blend or On Guard (DoTErra). Rub drops on bottom of feet 2-3 times per day.

- **COCONUT OIL** - to fight bacteria, viruses, and parasites and help heal wounds. Also a great natural "love balm"! Use coconut oil in high-heat cooking, as a moisturizer or natural lubricant, in baked goods, and in your hair.

- High-quality **TURMERIC SUPPLEMENT** to ease pain and reduce inflammation.

- **FRESH GINGER ROOT** – anti-inflammatory herb that supports digestion, relieves a sore throat and builds immune function. Cut an inch piece of root into slices and boil with water in a pot for 5 minutes. Sip on tea with a little honey.

- **BAKING SODA** for insect bites and bee stings. Add 1 Tbsp. baking soda with a little water to make a paste. Rub paste on insect bite or itchy areas.

- **HOMEOPATHIC REMEDIES**

- **APIS MELLIFICA 30C** to relieve swelling from insect bites or allergies (Dissolve 5 pellets under tongue 3x/day)

- **ARNICA** (30 C pellets or cream/ointment)– Relieves muscle pain, stiffness and swelling from bruises. Dissolve 5 pellets under tongue 3x/day

- **SEVEN ESSENTIAL OILS** – lavender, lemon, peppermint, frankincense, melaleuca (tea tree), digestive blend, protective blend (DoTerra - On Guard, Young Living - Thieves)

Hangover Helpers

Good morning Sunshine!

I'll spare the lecture on why overindulging is not recommended for long term health, or the damaging effects of alcohol on the liver because the truth is it happens to the best of us. Here are some worthy reminders to nurse that hangover naturally and feel better fast. It's not just how much you drink but **WHAT YOU DRINK**. Beer and cheap wine are highest in hangover toxins. Choose organic wine or go for high quality distilled spirits like tequila, vodka, gin, or scotch on the rocks or with mineral water. **(*Low carb, no sugar or gluten and some have antioxidants*)**. But skip the mixed drinks loaded with sugar!

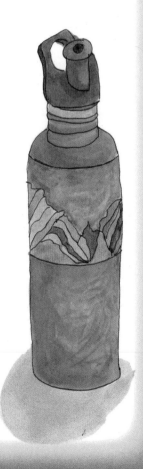

- **HYDRATE** - For every glass of alcohol have equal amounts of filtered or mineral water. If hungover, sip on cool water and add a sprinkle of unrefined sea salt, a squeeze of lemon or lime or 2 tsp. of apple cider vinegar to alkalize your blood.

- **KOMBUCHA** - fermented tea, right before bed. Alcohol depletes friendly bacteria and fermented foods are loaded with probiotics, B vitamins, and liver supporting detoxifiers, which might do the trick.

- Load up on **PROTEIN AND LEAFY GREENS** the morning after – like a green powder drink, fresh green juice, or eggs and spinach (with some raw sauerkraut!). Toxins hitch a ride out your body with proteins and the greens will support your liver.

- **FERMENTED FOODS** - Eat lots of cultured fermented foods - Raw pickles, naturally cultured sauerkraut, kimchi (Korean sauerkraut), real plain

whole fat yogurt, kombucha, or coconut kefir.

• **MORNING COFFEE** can stimulate and relieve headache pain but it's also very dehydrating so be sure to drink equal amounts of water.

• **TIGER BALM** for Headaches. This blend of camphor, menthol, cajuput oil and clove oil is known for its blood flowing properties and a great topical headache cure. Massage on the back of your neck and temples but keep away from your eyes or private parts, YIKES it stings!

• **YOGA POSE** - Try a seated or lying down yoga twist to wring the alcohol out of your organs. The perfect post-party liver purge.

• **REST** - Make sure to get plenty of rest today. Sleep in, take a nap and take it easy. You probably didn't sleep very well last night while your body was working hard to remove toxins.

Apple Cider Vinegar

I consume at least 1 Tbsp. of apple cider vinegar (ACV) every day to help my body become less acidic and more alkaline (see tip #1 below). Bacteria, viruses, fungus and cancers thrive in an acid environment. I also take it personally for improved digestion and for a quick burst of energy.

Make sure when buying apple cider vinegar you buy it raw and with the "mother" which means it still contains the beneficial compounds including probiotics. Apple cider vinegar can also be used for personal care—like conditioning hair, whitening teeth and as an overall camper cleaner.

The benefits of apple cider vinegar come from its powerful healing compounds, which include *acetic acid, potassium, magnesium, probiotics and enzymes.*

Acetic acid can kill dangerous "bad" bacteria, and also encourage growth of beneficial "good" bacteria. It essentially acts as a natural antibiotic. This means apple cider vinegar naturally provides numerous benefits related to skin, digestion, and immunity health without any side effects.

Nutrition Tip:

Benefits of Apple Cider Vinegar

- **Can reduce Acid Reflux and Heartburn** - Some of the main causes of acid reflux and heartburn are an imbalanced stomach pH and lack of hydrochloric acid, enzymes and probiotics. Apple cider vinegar is full of all of these nutrients. Adding 1 Tbsp. of apple cider vinegar (or swap this for 1 Tbsp. fresh lemon juice) to a cup of water and drinking it five minutes before meals can reduce symptoms and help relieve acid reflux.

- **Can Kill Candida (Yeast) and Boost Probiotics** - Many people struggle with candida and yeast. The side effects can be bad breath, lack of energy, UTI's and digestive issues. ACV contains probiotics and a type of acid that promotes the growth of probiotics, which help kill off candida. Remove sugar from your diet and consume 1 tbsp. of apple cider vinegar 3x daily as part of a candida cleanse.

- **High in potassium**. This mineral helps keep the arteries flexible and resilient. It helps fight off harmful bacteria and viruses and to dissolve fat. Most Americans are potassium deficient.

- **Soothe a Sunburn or bug bite** - Add ½ cup apple cider vinegar to a bowl of hot water. Add 1-2 Tbsp. coconut oil and a few drops of lavender essential oil. Using a washcloth, towel or cotton balls, rub generously on sunburnt or infected skin.

- **Heal Poison Oak or Poison Ivy** - The minerals in apple cider vinegar like potassium can help reduce swelling and inflammation, improving poison ivy. Also, ACV can help detox the poison out of your skin helping poison ivy heal more quickly. Use same recipe as sunburn remedy.

- **Help heal a Cold and Sore Throat** - Apple cider vinegar is the ultimate remedy to cure a cold and sore throat fast! Because it's loaded with vitamins and probiotic boosting acetic acid it's a great natural cure. Take 2 tablespoons of apple cider vinegar in one glass of water 3x daily to get rid of that cold.

Constipation

A lot of folks complain about constipation when traveling. Is it the foreign toilet, a different schedule, or not taking time to relax with your morning cup of coffee or tea to wait for the urge? Whatever the reason here are some natural tips to get things moving.

• Begin and/or end your day with **8 oz. warm water w/ 2tsp. apple cider vinegar or ½ lemon juiced.** Add a few drops of stevia if it's too tart – a natural sweetener or a little honey to alkalize your blood.

• **Probiotics are an important first step in treating constipation:** Take a high quality probiotic starting at ¼ tsp. daily, increase to ½ Tbsp. daily. Lacto-fermented foods such as yogurt, kefir, sauerkraut, and pickles also provide probiotics.

• **Prunes:** Soak prunes in water overnight, and eat 2-4 in the morning with soaking liquid.

• **Flax Seeds, organic:** Consume 2 Tbsp. of freshly ground organic flaxseeds once or twice daily, followed by a full glass of water. Flax seeds keep well in a jar or in the freezer.

• **Salt your food more generously:** Our bowels need salt for two reasons: it helps to hold water in the colon and it directly feeds the cells lining the GI tract. Enjoy your salt!

• **Optimize FIBER:** (50 grams or more). Fiber adds bulk to your stools. Top sources: raspberries, blueberries, strawberries, lentils, nuts, chia and 2 Tbsp. of freshly ground flax Seeds (2x/day), kale, quinoa, avocado, apples, winter squash, broccoli and celery!

• **Hydrate:** Make sure you drink enough water. Water and fiber make a nice sponge that will give you bulk. Drink half your body weight in ounces of water daily.

- **Try eliminating gluten:** One of the most constipating foods I've ever encountered is gluten. For many people, it is what it sounds like: "glue".

- **Exercise:** aerobic exercise in particular – stimulates bowel and lymphatic systems. So, do a brisk hike, jump rope, do some jumping jacks, or just go for a jog!

- **Squat:** easy in the great outdoors, especially if you're not close to an outhouse. Most cultures around the world squat when they move their bowels rather than sit on a toilet. This is actually structurally more conducive for your bowels to eliminate and will unkink your colon when you poop.

- **Try drinking hot coffee or peppermint tea** in the morning

- **Vitamin C flush:** utilize 2500mg of buffered vitamin C. Start with 2 caps (500mg each) or 1 tsp. of powdered vitamin C and work up if to 2500mg or until relief is achieved. Convenience stores or gas stations may carry Emergen-C. Mix 2 packets with water in the AM. Watch out for gas and stomach pain if dosage is increased too quickly. Do not use if you have or suspect an ulcer or other bowel disease, as it can be too hard on the GI tract. Use magnesium instead.

- **Magnesium citramate: (citrate and malate)** relaxes muscles. Start with 400 milligrams daily and increase as needed up to 600mg each night. Too much will cause diarrhea.

- **Take digestive enzymes:** Specifically protease for protein digestion and pancreatin (which has protease, amylase and lipase). Take 1-2 caps 30 minutes before or 20-60 minutes after a meal. This allows enzymes to make it into the intestinal tract instead of being destroyed with your meal.

- **Relax:** Digestion is a parasympathetic process. Be in a relaxed state, not a stress state, for it to function properly. Take a few deep breaths to shift into a parasympathetic mode and trust that your body can and will do what needs to be done.

Snake Bites

Snakebites from venomous and non-venomous snakes can cause long-lasting health problems and even death. Seeking proper medical treatment as soon as possible is imperative. When bitten by a snake, follow these guidelines:

- Remove tight clothing and jewelry before swelling begins.

- Remain calm and move away from the snake. They can, and will, strike again.

- Keep the bite area at or below the level of the heart.

- Clean the wound, but don't flush it with water.

- Do not use a tourniquet.

- Do not apply ice or heat.

- Apply a clean, dry bandage.

- Do not take any pain medication or allergy medication.

- Do not cut the wound or attempt to remove the venom.

- Avoid caffeine or alcohol, as this will speed the rate of absorption of the toxin.

- Keep as still as possible; carry the victim, if possible, to get help.

- Do not try to capture the snake; take a picture if it is safe to do so, or make a note of color, markings and shape of the head.

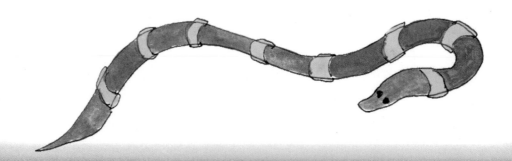

Natural Treatments to Relieve Symptoms of Snake Bites

1.   **Lavender Essential Oil:** getting bit by a snake can be very stressful. Remaining calm is essential, particularly when bitten by a venomous snake as an increased heart rate can cause the toxins to spread more quickly. Use a few drops of lavender essential oil behind the ears, or just sniff directly out of the bottle to speed relief.

2.   **Melaleuca oil (AKA Tea Tree Oil):** After a bite, clean the area thoroughly. Use natural antibacterial cleanser, like 3-4 drops melaleuca oil mixed with 1-2 drops coconut oil. Wrap with a clean dry bandage; do not wrap too tightly. Follow directions if 911 instructs you not to cleanse the area, particularly after a rattlesnake, copperhead, coral snake or water moccasin bite.

3.   **Coconut Oil:** fights bacteria, viruses, and parasites and has been shown to help heal wounds. Apply a small amount of coconut oil to the wound and wrap with a bandage to speed healing.

Insect Bites

mosquito bites, bee stings, spider bites

Homeopathy: Apis mellifica 30C to relieve swelling from insect bites or allergies. Dissolve 5 pellets under the tongue 3 times a day until symptoms are relieved.

Essential Oils: lavender, frankincense, lemon, melaleuca – use topically or add carrier oil like coconut or olive oil. (*3-4 drops essential oil to 1 tsp. carrier oil*)

Ice Cubes: wrap cubes in towel and press against bite for 10 minutes or as long as you can tolerate.

Tea bags: Natural tannins in tea (preferably black tea) work as an astringent, drawing toxins out of the skin and helps relieve discomfort from bites. Pressed used tea bag against skin until itching subsides.

Black & Orange beetle Death Valley 4-20-11

LADYBUG ON COREOPSIS

Baking Soda Paste: Add a few drops of water to baking soda to make a paste. Apply directory on skin and let it dry. The alkalinity of baking soda can neutralize the pH of infected area and relieve itching.

Apple cider vinegar: a swab of apple cider vinegar can help neutralize a bug bite and balance pH of infected area.

Essential Oils

Essential Oils are my go-to first aid kit. The bottles are small and potent so very easy to bring on the road. The main ways I use essential oils when camping is topically (with or without a carrier oil) or inhaling right from the bottle.

Topical Use: Some essential oils can be placed directly on the skin by rubbing a few drops on the bottom of each foot or directly on a targeted area. Some oils are very strong and can burn the skin so these should be mixed with a carrier oil.

Best carrier oils: coconut oil, almond oil, olive oil and jojoba oil. Mix 3-4 drops essential oil with 1 tsp. carrier oil. Apply behind ears, neck, abdomen, soles and tops of feet.

Ingestion: I do not recommend ingesting essential oils as they usually don't make it through the digestive track to the area you are trying to treat. Applying them topically or inhaling them is more effective. Oils recommended for internal use for digestive distress, like peppermint oil, can be massaged on the stomach and produce the same results. You could also place a drop of essential oil on the inside of the cheek allowing oils to absorbed slowing directly into the bloodstream.

These are the top seven oils and their benefits that I recommend bringing when on the road:

 MELALEUCA also known as tea tree oil has powerful antiseptic properties and is a great first aid for the skin. Dilute with carrier oil: 3-4 drops melaleuca to 1 tsp. carrier oil.

- Kills funguses and yeast (apply topically for athlete's foot and toe fungus)
- Heals gum disease – use topically on gums
- Antibacterial cleanser, Use topically with lavender to clean and disinfect wounds and rashes.

LAVENDER is well-known for its soothing, calming properties—can be applied directly to skin without a carrier oil.

- Relaxes body, reduces anxiety and relieves headaches.
- Heals skin and lip disorders, sunburn, wounds and burns around the campfire.
- Apply immediately to help calm bee stings or bug bites.
- Reduces high blood pressure and cholesterol.
- Relieves insomnia.
- Supports hormone balance.

PEPPERMINT may be the most versatile essential oil. Cool and invigorating!

- Improves focus, energy and concentration – inhale deeply!
- Supports digestion, reduces nausea, acid reflux and bloating
- Relieves muscle aches and pain
- Use with lemon to fight bad breath and odor

- Improves breathing by fighting respiratory and sinus infections – just rub directly on chest

- Add to filtered water in spray bottle and mist body when overheated (10 drops in a 1 ounce bottle of water)

LEMON is best known for it's ability to cleanse toxins from any part of the body

- Cleanses body and lymphatic system – apply topically behind ears and ankles to cleanse and balance pH.

- Add a drop to honey to soothe a dry sore throat.

- Rub topically over chest to relieve congestion and mucus

- Kills bad bacteria - add 10-15 drops to 1 cup water in spray bottle to clean kitchen counters and bathroom.

- Improves mood and reduces anxiety

- **Used for a bug repellant** (I also use DoTerra Terra Shield oil for a bug repellant)

FRANKINCENSE, also known as Boswellia, is one of the most underrated and most powerful essential oil in the world.

- Fights cancer and Boosts immune system – massage 1 or 2 drops on bottom of feet

- Reduces inflammation and fights infections – apply to bottom of feet.

- Improves depression and mood – add 1 drop under tongue (food grade only oils)

- Spiritual awareness – apply under nose and back of neck.

- Heals skin scarring, sunspots and acne – apply topically to wounds or wrinkles

PROTECTIVE BLEND - a blend of essential oils that has tremendous healing properties. (***Clove, Orange, Cinnamon, Eucalyptus and Rosemary***) I use ***DoTerra Brand*** essential oils and they named their protective blend "On Guard." ***Young Living*** makes one called "Thieves."

- Fights off colds and flu - apply 1–2 drops directly to bottom of feet

- Disinfectant against bacteria and germs - dilute 10 drops with 1 cup water and spray on surfaces

- Anti-inflammatory – apply to bottom of feet or for Urinary Tract Infection rub on lower abdomen

- Supports immune system – rub on bottom of feet

- Opens sinuses and improve allergy symptoms – apply topically diluted with carrier to chest and sinuses.

✿

DIGESTIVE BLEND (Ginger, Peppermint, Fennel)

- Reduces nausea and stomach cramps – apply on stomach

- Improves acid reflux - take internally with lemon and water (food grade oil only)

- Anti-inflammatory – rub on bottom of feet

- Treats IBS, diarrhea and constipation - add a few drops in water and take internally (food grade oil only)

- Freshens breath – add to water and gargle

Expansive Yoga

Practicing yoga in an expansive landscape like on the edge of the Ubehebe Crater in Death Valley expands my body, mind and perspective. This winter day we hiked around the whole crater—something we would never attempt in the hot summer.

Back to the Land

The art of healing comes from nature, not from the physician. Therefore the physician must start from nature, with an open mind.
–Paracelsus

Little did I realize that reading the book **Back to the Land** in 1970 would make a lasting impression on my future. It was one of the first books I devoured on self-sufficient living and it inspired my dream to grow our own food, raise chickens and goats, build a house and live in harmony with the rhythms of nature.

In reaction to industrialization and crowded cities, there have been many back-to-the-land movements as societies search for a happier, healthier and simpler life. Concerns about urban problems of over-consumerism, air and water pollution and failings of government inspired people like me to connect with the basics of nature and learn practical survival skills not dependent on city life.

Bill and I quickly realized that self-sufficiency in the true sense was a lot more work than we wanted to pursue – especially while still young and building our family and careers. However, we managed to buy land and build our house (it only took about 20 years), but our earlier dream of raising animals made us feel too tied down to our land. We wanted time to travel with our family and explore the untamed territories across the States.

Along with my desire to live a simpler life in the country, I was drawn to learn natural healing remedies for digestion, building immunity and treating injuries. Although raising two children as a stay–at-home mom was probably more work than I had imagined, I found time to grow an awesome vegetable garden and discover everything I could about the art of natural healing.

Believe me, I am not against modern medicine. My family and I are extremely grateful for the precision and speed of occasional drugs used to tackle a particular disease or emergency. But most drugs are toxic to our body if over-consumed, so I try to use modern medicine only when a disease or injury is life-threatening or incurable by natural methods.

My first line of defense to my health is prevention. I treat my body, mind and spirit as one (holistic) and refer to them as a package deal. The foundation of traditional or alternative medicine begins with a healthy diet, exercise, restful sleep and spending time in nature!

Throughout years of exploring the great outdoors, our camping trips today have practically transformed into "glamping" experiences. Glamping is described as a style of camping where nature meets modern luxury. We have discovered how to live quite comfortably in the wild away from home.

Lower Calf Creek Falls, Grand Staircase-Escalante, Utah

My intention is to inspire folks to get outside; explore this beautiful country; prepare delicious, whole food meals; learn natural healing remedies to treat common camping ailments, and practice simple yoga postures to stay limber on your camping adventure. I hope this book becomes a treasured companion to ensure that vibrant health and healing can flourish with the gifts of nature.

Adopt the pace of nature: her secret is patience.

12
Yoga at the Rest Stop

Yoga at the Rest Stop
transform that "highway coma"

Isn't yoga a spiritual practice done in a quiet place with candles and soft music?

Well – that depends. . . where you are.

The cool thing about this ancient discipline is that Yoga can be practiced in-numerous ways.... Some folks do physical postures to create a beautiful toned and relaxed body. Others find peace and contentment with daily breath work and meditation. Several follow the path of sound through chanting and mantras to access higher states of consciousness. And I like practicing in nature or even at a rest stop while traveling.

No matter how it's interpreted, Yoga invites us to become still and listen to our body, mind and heart. It doesn't matter where you are. You can create a sanctuary within by simply pausing. . . take a few deep breaths . . . find stillness . . . and "check in with your SELF".

Remember how you feel after driving for 2-3 hours?

Your mind's in a trance and your body has a hard time standing up straight-when you finally stop to take a break. A few deep belly breaths and mindful stretches on a picnic table can be an amazing way to swap that "highway coma" for mental clarity and a more flexible body.

Today yoga has become an integral part of Western society. Yoga Journal Magazine estimates that about 8.7% or 20 million Americans practice some form of yoga today. I believe this resurgence reflects a deep yearning to re-connect with our sacred selves.

I discovered yoga in college about the same time I was beginning to question my very existence. I felt like I had found my church and my people in that first yoga class. But this church was within and what I had been seeking was a sense of wholeness through my body, mind and spirit. After class I didn't feel spaced out or in a trance (like I imagined yoga to be)– I felt totally ALIVE with acute mental clarity and freedom in my physical body.

The word YOGA comes from Sanskrit meaning, "to yoke or unite". Yoga unites our body, mind, emotions and spirit through postures, breath work, medita-tion and understanding yoga philosophy. It helps us understand, accept and feel comfortable with ourselves.

Most folks enter this spiritual practice through the physical postures. Once we cross that threshold we open ourselves to let go and look within to under-stand that we are not just our bodies, minds or emotions. We discover that we are all Divine Beings and have the ability to live our lives with peace, joy and love.

Can we find happiness by practicing yoga at the rest stop?

You bet!!!! Get over any embarrassment! Sitting for hours can be one of the biggest insults on our body as we become stiff, cranky and inflexible! I guar-antee you'll feel so much better after doing a few postures before driving the last leg of your journey. Instead of arriving at your campsite exhausted, why not feel excited to set up camp and enjoy time off.

Yoga Poses with Bench

Take some deep breaths and try just 2 or 3 of these poses at the rest stop, campground, on top of the mountain, inside your camper or against a tree. I guarantee you'll feel more connected to your self and a lot happier too!

Yoga is NOT about self improvement, it's about self acceptance and discovery

Down Dog on Bench

Place hands on bench and take a big step back, feet hip distance apart. Bend knees and draw hips back. Start to straighten legs as much as possible. Down dog can also be done with hands on table for an easier variation.

BENEFITS: Elongates spine. Opens legs and arms.

Up Dog

Wiggle feet back a little and bring shoulders forward over wrists (plank position) and drop hips even more and bring heart forward. Go back and forth between down dog and up dog 3 times.

BENEFITS: Awakens entire body, Strengthens arms and opens chest. Very invigorating!

Lunge on Bench

1. Place right foot on bench and wiggle left foot back until you feel a good stretch in your strong, firm left leg.

2. Bend your right leg to a 90° angle with knee right over ankle. Release deeply in your front leg while drawing the right hip back a bit.

3. Lift your heart and breathe.

4. While holding pose bend back left leg slightly until you feel a good stretch in left front groin, hip flexor and psoas. Switch sides.

BENEFITS: Opens psoas and hip flexor of back leg. Stretches hamstring. Great if you've been sitting (driving).

Lunge Twist on Bench

2 variations

1. With right foot on bench in lunge leave left hand on bench on inside of right foot.

2. Place right hand on hip.

3. Draw right hip back, keep right knee over right ankle.

4. Leave right hand on hip or extend it at a diagonal along right ear. Look up under armpit. Hold for 3-5 breaths.

Variation #2: Bring left elbow to outside of right knee. Lengthen through crown of head and rotate torso to right. Breathe. Switch sides.

BENEFITS: Stretches leg muscles. Lengthens and aligns spine. Relieves stiffness in neck and shoulders.

Hamstring Stretch Variations

Place right foot on bench with both legs straight. Check standing foot and make sure it's pointing straight forward. Keep standing leg firm to anchor the posture. If hamstrings are tight, bend right leg slightly. Try to fold forward but if too tight remain standing and keep legs firm. Don't fall over; this is balancing pose!

BENEFITS: Major hamstring stretch that strengthens ankles and concentration.

Another Hamstring Stretch!

Stand facing table. Lift one leg and rest your foot on top of table. When balance feels steady (find a drishti) and standing leg strong, lift both arms overhead. Keeps legs firm reaching hands toward sky.

Breathe. . . . Switch sides.

BENEFITS: Strengthens ankles leg muscles, core and concentration. Opens hamstrings, spine and shoulders

Side Body Hamstring Stretch
(or just another form of triangle pose)

1.   Standing with left side facing table, lift left leg on top of table, toes pointing up.

2.   Make sure right foot is pointing straight forward on ground or parallel to table. Begin with your left hand on our hip and right arm at side.

3.   Find your balance and a drishti.

4.   Dynamically lift right arm up towards sky, palm facing inward. Tighten your right kneecap (without locking your knee) and stretch your whole right side.

5.   Gradually start to bend sideways toward left foot reaching left had to ankle or hold on to foot if you can reach. Feel the incredible stretch on your right side and left hamstring.

6.   Lift your heart and reach through the crown of your head. If comfortable feeling balanced, begin to twist the torso to the right lifting your heart and your gaze toward the sky.

7.   Breathe. . . 5 deep breaths. Switch sides.

".... Breathe deep of that yet sweet and lucid air, sit quietly for a while and contemplate the precious stillness, the lovely mysterious, and awesome space."

-Edward Abbey

Hamstring and Hip Stretch: (Parsvotanasana)

1. With legs parted 2–2.5 feet apart and hips facing forward, turn back foot in 45–60 degrees. Feet are not lined up in a straight line (you're standing on two imaginary narrow railroad tracks)

2. If hips and hamstrings are tight take a shorter stance (moving legs closer together). Bend front leg as needed. Keep back heel down while turning hips to front. Try folding forward with hands on bench.

3. If more flexible bring hands down to ground.

BENEFITS: Opens hamstrings, hips, calves, ankles and lower back.

Seated Hip Opener

1. Sit on bench, legs wide, feet pointing straight forward. Bring elbows to knees and lift heart.

2. Try bending forward and extend arms to stretch back and open hips. Take 5 breaths.

BENEFITS: Opens hips, hamstrings making it easier to squat in woods.

Modified King Dancer Pose
(or Intense quadriceps stretch)

1.   Stand next to table or a tree (hold on to these props if balance is shaky).

2.   Standing firm on your left leg, grab your right foot with right hand behind you. Reach left arm up toward sky. Feel the incredible stretch on your left side and on the front of your right quadriceps and psoas.

3.   Keep your focus (and balance) by staring at a **drishti** * or if you're daring, look up toward the sky.

4.   5 breaths here. Switch sides.

Drishti - (view or gaze) a specific focal point while holding a yoga posture. The ancient yogis discovered when the gaze is fixed on a single point the mind is diminished from being stimulated by all other external objects and balance and concentration are strengthened.

BENEFITS: While hiking or sitting all day in a car our quadriceps and psoas can get very tight. This posture opens the front body and helps us stand taller!

Tree Pose

I'm kind of a show off when it comes to Tree Pose.

I love to burst into this posture when I arrive at the top of a mountain, the top of a rock, or balancing on the rim of the Grande Canyon!!!!

1.   If your balance is questionable, stand next to a picnic table or tree and hold on with one hand.

2.   Standing firmly on one leg, lift your other leg to the inside of your thigh (or calf or your ankle).

3.   Press your foot into your thigh and press your inner thigh into the opposite foot.

4.   Keep hands on hips, in prayer position at heart or raise both arms up overhead and into a "V" formation.

5.   Find your "drishti", spread your fingers, root down into the earth and SMILE!

BENEFITS:

Strengthens legs and core, opens hips and shoulders and gives a beautiful upward stretch and sense of balance.

[Tree pose near Escalante, Utah]

Tree pose can even be practiced as a partner pose.

Even though my son Logan is 6'3", we managed to balance together in front of the Tetons on a very smoky day. Be sure to switch sides!

Balance postures help strengthen your ankles, legs and core but also give us confidence while navigating the backcountry.

You never know when you need to cross a creek on a log, stand up on a boat or SUP (Stand Up Paddle board) or scale a narrow wall in a slot canyon.

I practice balancing poses all the time to keep my ankles and knees strong too!

"Yoga does not transorm the way we see things, it transforms the person who sees."

-B.K.S. Iyengar

Postures on Picnic Table

If you brought a yoga mat place it on top of table. A large towel will work too.

Reclined Butterfly

Lying on your back, bring both knees toward chest and put soles of the feet together. Reach between your knees and grab your ankles or feet. Draw your feet toward your head and press your knees away. Drop your tailbone and broaden your collarbones.

BENEFITS: Increases blood flow to abdomen, pelvis and hips. Keeps sexual organs healthy.

Thread the Needle

Begin lying down, knees bent with both feet flat on the mat. Cross outside of right ankle on top of left thigh. Reach your right hand through your legs and clasp your both hands behind the left thigh. Flex right foot, press lower back down and broaden your collarbones. Breathe 3-5 breaths.

BENEFITS: One of the best ways to open the hips and lengthen the spine.

Reclined Leg Stretch Series
Supta Padagustasana

Practice the following postures on the right leg and then switch to left leg.

Reclined Leg Stretch
(*Supta Padagustasana*)

Using a strap around right foot straighten it toward the sky. Hold on to strap with both hands and relax shoulders. Reach through both heels, and keep left leg firm. If hamstrings are tight keep right knee slightly bent.

BENEFITS: Relieves stiffness in lower back and sciatic pain. Lengthens hamstrings of top leg and quadriceps of bottom leg.

Reclined Leg to Side Stretch

With strap around your foot rotate your right leg out to the side and let it hover over the table. Keep left leg strong and focus on keeping left hip on the table. Externally rotate right foot so toes point down, heel up. Breathe and hold for 3-5 breaths. Bring right leg back to center, release strap and bend both knees, feet flat on the table.

BENEFITS: Opens pelvis and chest. Stretches inner hamstring and inner knee.

Reclined Table Twist

With feet flat on table lift hips and shift to the right a few inches. Lower hips down and cross right thigh over left thigh and roll to the left. You can put your left hand on knee to invite it down but keep right shoulder on the table. Keep right arm at side or increase the stretch by placing

right arm on table next to right ear. Breathe...5 deep breaths.

BENEFITS: Opens outside hip of top leg. Brings broadness to back muscles by allowing gravity to open your spine. Keep your right shoulder on the floor as you focus on surrendering.

Knees to Chest, Ankles Crossed

Before practicing the last 5 postures on the left side hug both knees to chest and cross your ankles. Rock side to side to bring your hips back to neutral and relax your sacrum.

BENEFITS: Opens the glutes and lower back.

Savasana

Deep Relaxation

This is the most important pose of the whole practice.

1.   If lying flat on your back doesn't work, bend both knees, feet flat on the table. Separate feet a bit wider and turn them pigeon toe.

2.   Allow knees to fall together.

3.   Cover yourself with a towel or blanket if feeling chilled.

4.   A few deep breaths and allow yourself to completely relax for at least 5 minutes or more.

"Yesterday I was clever so I wanted to change the world.
Today I am wise so I am changing myself."

–Rumi

Savasana – Awakening to Oneness

Savasana or "corpse pose" is the final deep relaxation pose of a yoga practice. It's a sacred time to assimilate all the benefits of the physical yoga postures and is usually done lying down in stillness for 5-15 minutes. When weather conditions are just right, lying on top of a picnic table in savasana can be heavenly!

The first time I experienced savasana in a yoga class back in 1971, I didn't have the vocabulary to describe how I was feeling. I was in a blissful state with 20 other students lying on our mats in complete stillness. For ten minutes, no words were spoken; only deep relaxation as an awakening of peace and tranquility was felt among kindred spirits.

As my yoga journey evolved I realized I was experiencing a feeling of *"Oneness"*. I felt connected to something greater than myself, like an invisible golden thread merging with all living things. This "spiritual connection" is actually a 'state of being' and can intensify while camping and spending time in nature:

A difficult hike erupts into a beautiful 360 degree view

While kayaking, we pause and breathe the fresh ocean breeze

Driving becomes exhilarating through pelting rain, wind and hail

Fellow travelers offer kindness and help with directions

A herd of wild elk run swiftly across the highway

On a chilly night we huddle with kindred spirits around a campfire

Incredible flavors and recipes are savored while eating outdoors

As human beings we all have similar emotions and needs. I encourage you to seek harmony and "oneness" through exploring our great outdoors; yoga or any mindfulness practice. The benefits of this spiritual practice will affect how you live and how you relate to others.

We really are *"One Human Tribe"* practicing harmony on this great planet.

Katie and dogs (Ginger & Chilli), Alabama Hills

Acknowledgments

This legendary cookbook began when Bill and I became empty nesters and camping trips were a respite from our hectic work schedules. I found time to journal and record my feelings and insights of the world around me. On the road I began creating recipes for campfire meals. I sketched stick figure yoga sequences to practice on the picnic table. I knew I had settled into a relaxed state when I began to draw and slow down to curiously study my surroundings. It was my meditation and way of being in the present moment.

This book came together on those healing trips. It evolved as an expression of this adventurous time in our lives while we're still fit enough to withstand the joys and hardships of camping and explore the vast wilderness.

There are many amazing people to acknowledge who have encouraged and contributed to the birth of this creation.

Thank you to all my nutrition and yoga students who inspired me to keep learning and sharing. Thank you for testing my recipes and assuring me they were not only healthy but also tasty and fairly easy to make too! Thank you yoginis for practicing chair yoga as if it were a picnic table.

Deep gratitude to my writing and editing coaches.

Molly Fisk my first coach – you inspired me to write from my heart and keep journaling daily. Thanks for referring me to Maxima Kahn.

Maxima Kahn – you were my life force for many months when I felt this project was overwhelming. Your guided meditations brought me back to "why" I was writing this book and focus on my top priorities. Your suggestion for a spirit guide was simply superb. I held Elk Medicine close to my heart; remembering to pace myself whenever I felt impatient or close to burnout. You understood the underlying message of my book, and your edits felt aligned with my style. Your enthusiasm for my artwork gave me confidence to keep drawing.

Vail Kobbe and Virginia Lee – for your thoughtful edits and encouragement to keep writing.

Julie Valin – my graphic artist extraordinaire and book designer. You made my artwork and recipes look professional, easy to read and a joy to just browse through this colorful book. You inspired me to draw even more and as the saying goes practice makes perfect. I had a purpose and with your guidance, drawing became a lot of fun and improved through time. Thank you for your creative edits and enjoyable personality to work with.

Thank you photographers – Bill Carter, Jenna Stratton, Nam Fon Carter and David Heaton for your keen perspectives.

My indexer – Greg Jewett, thank you!

And to all my friends and family who are my biggest cheerleaders! Thank you for your support and encouragement along this journey.

My husband Bill Carter – for your love of camping adventures and instilling a deep appreciation for the great outdoors. Dad is smiling at how well you take care of me - especially assuring my comfort while camping. You are always my greatest recipe critic!

Thad Nodine – your writing experience and suggestions helped me focus on the bigger picture of publishing a book.

Nam Fon Carter – your creative Thai cooking has influenced many recipes and your presentation is exquisite!

Our sons Noel and Logan Carter – for all the camping memories past and present that feed our souls and life long heart connection.

Martha Meredith – your travel journals inspired me to be CREATIVE, whimsical and have fun drawing and writing.

Connie Coale – your friendship, encouragement and belief in me has propelled forward motion of my dream.

David and Patt Lind Kyle – your writing, publishing and wise marketing experience helped me make the decision to self publish!

Wendy and Corbett Riley – for all the amazing camping adventures with some wild and crazy friends!

About the Author

Katie Carter loves to cook.

Watch out! Her enthusiasm and boundless energy for creating and sharing recipes is contagious. Certified as a nutrition consultant and yoga teacher, Katie inspires us to eat healthy meals and keep our bodies strong and limber, even when traveling. When not in her kitchen, she loves to garden, make art, teach nutrition and yoga classes, or explore the great outdoors with her husband Bill. Her nutritional knowledge and passion for healthy living will ignite your camping and eating experience to another level. Katie lives with Bill on 5 acres in Nevada City, CA.

Index

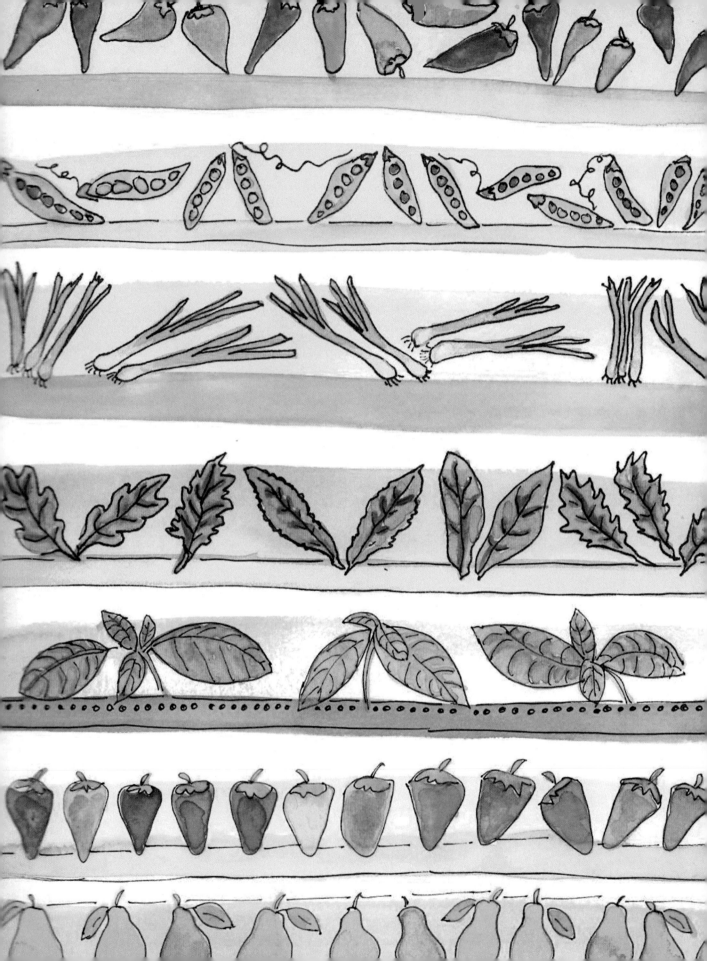

47279661R00136